# Keegstra

P9-BJA-021

# Keegstra

## The Trial, The Issues, The Consequences

Steve Mertl
and
John Ward

Western Producer Prairie Books
Saskatoon, Saskatchewan

Copyright © 1985 by Steve Mertl and John Ward
Western Producer Prairie Books
Saskatoon, Saskatchewan

All rights reserved. No part of this publication may be reproduced,
stored in a retrieval system, or transmitted, in any form or by any
means, electronic, mechanical, photocopying, recording, or otherwise,
without the prior written permission of the publisher.

Cover illustration courtesy CP Photo Service
Cover Design by Warren Clark, GDL

Printed in Canada by Modern Press ⬤1
Saskatoon, Saskatchewan

Western Producer Prairie Books publications are produced and
manufactured in the middle of western Canada by a unique
publishing venture owned by a group of prairie farmers who are
members of Saskatchewan Wheat Pool. From the first book in 1954, a
reprint of a serial originally carried in the weekly newspaper, *The
Western Producer,* to the book before you now, the tradition of
providing enjoyable and informative reading for all Canadians is
continued.

Canadian Cataloguing in Publication Data
Mertl, Steve, 1953-
 Keegstra

 Includes index.
 ISBN 0-88833-177-0
 1. Keegstra, Jim — Trials, litigation, etc.
 2. Antisemitism — Alberta.   3. Trials (Hate propaganda) —
 Alberta.   4. Teaching, Freedom of — Alberta.
 5. Freedom of speech — Alberta.   I. Ward, John,
 1952-      II. Title.
KE229K43M47 1985     345.71'0256     C85-091476-0

*To Madeleine and Kristin, for their patience*

CAMROSE LUTHERAN COLLEGE
LIBRARY

# Contents

# Preface

Jean-Paul Sartre, in a 1944 essay on the subject, said anti-Semitism is not an idea. It is a passion, and as such can not be divorced from the otherwise good qualities a person might possess, such as kindness and generosity. The point, made in a frank discussion about the anti-Semitic leanings of Sartre's French countrymen under German occupation, goes to the heart of the book you are about to read.

Jim Keegstra is, by all accounts, a caring, generous, Christian man. Not a saint, perhaps, but certainly a pillar of his community, the small central Alberta town of Eckville. How then can a person reconcile this picture with the one painted of Jim Keegstra at his trial on a charge of wilfully promoting hatred against the Jewish people, that of an obsessive, narrow-minded bigot whose world view was anchored to the belief Jews are at the root of civilization's problems?

The question is troubling and remains unanswered. Keegstra's longtime friends and acquaintances in the town of Eckville, at least those who perhaps don't subscribe to his views, were caught in that dilemma. Their unwillingness to reject the whole man for one facet of his character was perhaps understandable. After all, what do the man's feelings about Jews have to do with his helping me crop my hay field or rebuild my automobile engine? But to outsiders, and to many of his neighbors who saw the scope of his teachings for the first time during the trial, his anti-Semitism has poisoned the man, tipped the scales heavily off balance. He may not be ostracized, but he will not be regarded in quite the same way again.

This book is not about a one-dimensional, cardboard bigot who passed his hatred on to hundreds of young people who trusted him. It is about the human being we would find if we met Jim Keegstra face to face, for that is what he is. This is not an apology for what he did or what he stands for but a warning that stereotyping him or others like him might make us complacent, believing we can easily pick out the Keegstras in the crowd. We can not. Keegstra escaped detection for years. Historian Hannah Arendt spoke of "the banality of evil" in describing the workings of Nazi Germany, ordinary people doing monstrous things, things which seem like a dream now to those who did not witness them.

The Keegstra and Zundel cases came to trial in the 40th year after the downfall of the Nazi regime. They were framed in television and print retrospectives on the horror of those years. Suddenly, Canadians had living examples of the thinking which had led to the Holocaust. The story is by no means over. As this is written, appeals are expected in both cases. Keegstra is planning a trip to Europe to visit concentration camps, finally to see for himself. The hand remains to be played out.

We hope this book can provide some insight into the man and an introduction to the issues. We have not attempted to rebut much of the twisted history which Keegstra taught his students. We leave it to the reader to subject the material to the test for truth, a test Keegstra stressed highly but never seemed able to employ himself—that of contradiction.

# Acknowledgments

The authors wish to acknowledge the help of several individuals in the preparation of this book. First and foremost is Tony Gilroy, vice-president of marketing for The Canadian Press, without whose help there would be no book. Mike Williams, our editor, quickly absorbed the concept and smoothed the work. We would also like to thank Ross Henderson of the Red Deer *Advocate*, Bob Warwick of the *Calgary Herald* and Dick Gordon of CBC radio, who covered the Keegstra affair from its beginnings and provided us with useful ideas and guidance. We also appreciate the help received from other *Advocate* staff members.

Lastly we wish to acknowledge the co-operation of Jim Keegstra, who made time for us when other things were on his mind.

**281.2** (1) Every one who, by communicating statements in any public place, incites hatred against any identifiable group where such incitement is likely to lead to a breach of the peace, is guilty of

(a) an indictable offence and is liable to imprisonment for two years; or

(b) an offence punishable on summary conviction.

(2) Every one who, by communicating statements, other than in private conversation, wilfully promotes hatred against any identifiable group is guilty of

(a) an indictable offence and is liable to imprisonment for two years; or

(b) an offence punishable on summary conviction.

(3) No person shall be convicted of an offence under subsection (2)

(a) if he establishes that the statements communicated were true;

(b) if, in good faith, he expressed or attempted to establish by argument an opinion on a religious subject;

(c) if the arguments were relevant to any subject of public interest, the discussion of which was for the public benefit, and if, on reasonable grounds he believed them to be true; or

(d) if, on good faith, he intended to point out, for the purpose of removal, matters producing or tending to produce feelings of hatred towards an identifiable group in Canada.

*Criminal Code of Canada*

IN THE COURT OF
QUEEN'S BENCH OF ALBERTA
Judicial District of Red Deer
Her Majesty the Queen
Against
James Keegstra

James Keegstra stands charged that he, between
the 1st day of September A.D. 1978 and the 31st
day of December A.D. 1982 inclusive, at or near
the Town of Eckville in the Province of Alberta
did wilfully promote hatred against an identifiable group, to wit: the Jewish people, by communicating statements while teaching to students
at Eckville high school, contrary to the provisions
of the Criminal Code.

# 1

# As It Was
# In The Beginning

---

*A truth that's told with bad intent, beats all the lies you can invent.*

—William Blake

---

On warm September afternoons, as students just back to school fidgeted with memories of a summer gone by, Jim Keegstra would discuss the Problem of Truth. It was his traditional start to the social studies classes he taught at Eckville Junior-Senior High School. It was a good way to begin, to wean the students' minds from thoughts of summer jobs, evening cruising and the beer parties down by Hanson's Dam. Keegstra told his students to beware of contradictions, because contradiction is the hallmark of error. He said if the facts don't fit the theory, then the theory is wrong and has to be changed. He urged them to seek out different opinions and scrutinize alternatives.

It was a popular class. It was considered an easy course and Keegstra was an interesting teacher who kept the class lively with discussions and jokes.

In September 1981 there were 11 students in Keegstra's Grade 12 social studies classes. The whole school had only about 180 students, drawn from the community of Eckville itself, population 800, and the surrounding area of central Alberta, about halfway between Edmonton and Calgary.

The Grade 12 class was a close-knit group. There was Danny

Desrosiers, the star athlete, Dana Remillard, who would be named Queen of Hearts at the annual school ball and who would also be one of three class valedictorians, and the cheerful and popular Gwen Matthews. The class shared common interests and pastimes. They raced their cars on dusty backroads, drank beer, pursued romances, swam and hiked and talked and danced.

Their school was an old building, part wood-frame, part cinder block. Different parts were built as need dictated, giving the school a makeshift air. The most noticeable feature was the big, cinder-block gymnasium, home to a championship girls' basketball team and, when decorated with streamers and balloons, scene of school dances.

Their teacher was a popular man, well-liked by his students, respected by the community. He was mayor of the town and a pillar of his small, fundamentalist church. He was known as an honest, straightforward man, a God-fearing, straight-laced fellow who didn't smoke or drink. He wasn't much of a mixer, although he'd stop and chat down at the curling rink. His colleagues admired his teaching skills and the way he maintained a loose, but careful, discipline in his classes. He might abandon the day's lesson for a discussion of current events, but he brooked no rowdiness in class and his students knew where the line was drawn.

*This picture of Eckville High School illustrates the addition that was completed following Keegstra's dismissal. Ironically, James Keegstra presided over the opening of the new wing in his capacity as mayor of Eckville. (Canadian Press photo)*

Although Keegstra did not socialize much with the towns-people, he did spend a lot of time with their children. The students knew him as a man they could turn to for help and advice on anything, not just schoolwork. He was more than just a teacher and an authority figure, he was a friend. He was always willing to hang around after school to shoot the breeze. He was a good mechanic, too, and his willingness to roll up his sleeves and plunge into the greasy innards of an ailing engine endeared him to the boys. In a rural community a car is as much a part of a young man's life as girls and beer, and Keeg-stra's help in keeping the wheels turning was deeply appre-ciated.

"I would call him a good friend," said Desrosiers.

Keegstra's social studies class was as popular as the teacher. The students said it was interesting and challenging. He told them things they had never heard before. He made them think.

The teacher knew his stuff. He always had facts and figures to back his argument. In fact, the students said he never lost an argument. He knew the Bible too, cover to cover. There was a distinct biblical air about the classroom as Keegstra stressed Christian values and principles. As he taught, almost like a preacher, one student said, you knew that God was more than just a distant deity to Keegstra.

The curriculum for social studies in Alberta is pretty much wide open. There is a list of topics for discussion in class, but the teacher has a lot of leeway. Keegstra didn't use accepted sources for his classes. He told his students conventional his-tory books had a lot of lies in them, so he used the texts he trusted from his own library. He'd collected articles, books, tracts and pamphlets over years of "historical research" and they were what he used in teaching social studies. He said there was a monolithic conspiracy abroad in the world, which cen-sored history and produced misleading accounts for its own evil ends. Keegstra wasn't going to be a party to that and neither were his students.

So he lectured and wrote material on the blackboard and the students listened and copied it down. It was the basis for tests and essays required for the course. Shirley Nelson used her class notes to write an essay which said, in part: "Since the time before Christ, the Jews have been involved in all kinds of underhanded dealings. In 1783, they joined hands with the Communists to establish a one-world order." She got a mark of 85 per cent from Keegstra.

Holly French used her notes to write: "From 1936 to 1945, Hitler did a lot to try and rid the world of Bolsheviks. At least he tried to help our world by getting rid of the Jews instead of getting sucked into their socialist trap like people are now." She got an 85 too.

Keegstra's ideas were new to the students and some found them a little hard to follow. "It was very deep," Matthews was to say later. "There was a lot of it to understand."

He taught that a Jewish conspiracy had manipulated history for hundreds of years, moving behind the scenes, twisting people and nations to their own purpose, which is to destroy Christianity and bring about a single world government. He told them Jews are not really Jews. The Hebrews of the Bible were all but destroyed by the Romans and modern Jewry is descended from an obscure tribe called the Khazars, which converted to Judaism. Keegstra blamed almost every disaster in history on the Jews. They started the French Revolution, the American Civil War, both world wars and the Depression. They were Bolsheviks and Communists, socialists and capitalists.

"I challenge anybody to prove me wrong," he said one day. "Ninety-nine per cent of all finance is controlled by Jews."

It was a common challenge. He was always ready to throw down the gauntlet and defend his thesis. The students discussed things with him, but no one ever won a point. As far as Keegstra was concerned, conventional reference books contained "junk" and "garbage" and were useless in countering his views.

"I asked him how he could be sure his information was correct when there were so many textbooks that had conflicting views," recalled Charles Daniel. "He said we should research the author's background."

While there might be room for discussion and while Keegstra urged students to seek other sources in their research, the test answers and essays had to come straight from his teaching. It was the conspiracy theory or nothing. Efforts to hand in opposing views got short shrift.

One girl used an encyclopedia to prepare an essay on Bolshevism. It earned her a grade of 55 per cent and the comment penned on her paper: "Where did you get this? Built up by the Jewish press."

Another student, also using an encyclopedia, wrote that Czar Nicholas II bears part of the blame for the disastrous Russo-Japanese war of 1905. She too got 55 per cent and the scathing remark: "Where did you get this garbage? What about British and Jewish perfidy?"

The students' notebooks chronicle the classroom fixation with the Jews. Amid the usual doodles and sketches are blasé notations: "(Oliver) Cromwell had one fault, he believed in religious freedom and therefore he let in Jews." Other notes record that Jews used the word *goyim* to denote non-Jews and that "goyim" means dog. There are diagrams comparing evil Jewish socialism and Christian free enterprise.

The ideas Keegstra taught were condensed in the essays, but the basic pattern was true throughout. Jews were to blame for everything and the world would be a better place without them. The students had warm words for Hitler in their essays and several advocated getting rid of the Jews. One student said he simply wrote what he felt the teacher wanted to hear.

Richard Denis wrote a typical essay for Keegstra, entitled "The World Menace Since 1776." The menace was, of course, the Jewish-orchestrated conspiracy. The solution? Get rid of them.

Following is the Denis essay, complete with spelling errors and grammatical mistakes, none of which Keegstra noted or corrected. The comments Keegstra did add are noted in the body of the essay:

## The World Menace Since 1776

Since 1776, the World should be aware that we are slowly losing our freedom. The advancement of Communism and Socialism since this time has been tremendous. Inch by inch, second by second, the evil force behind this disease, dreaded by every free man, are taking over the world.

In this essay I will show you how the virus of this disease consists of one kind of people. The Jews since 1776 have financed and supported the spread of Communism because it is a step toward what they must feel is heaven. There heaven would be a New World Order under a One World Government. This government, of course, would be led by these cutthroats themselves with us as their "slaves." I wish to prove this.

The best place to start will be with a ruthless cutthroat known to the world as Adam Weishapt. He himself was a jesuit but disliked the church so he broke away from it when he was 25-30 years old. In 1771 Adam Weishapt disappeared mysteriously until May 1st 1776. (Incidentally, this date is said to be Satan's birthday) During these five years, Adam Weishapt had been writing of a plan in which he was going to take over. This plan was based on deseption and was made up of five points.

These five points are as follows. a) destruction of all Monarchy and legal government. b) destroy all religions—especially Christianity. c) abolish marriage (children raised by the state). d) abolish private property (land) and all inheritances. e) abolish all loyalty and allegence.

This plan is now the plan of all socialist and capitalist countries. It is the plan being followed behind the present day Iron curtain.

Adam Weishapt, after this plan organized a secret society. This organization was called the "Illuminaty" which means the enlightenment. His symbol for this organization is the same symbol used for communist countries. The five pointed Red Star. It was the Illuminaty which was behind the French Revolution. In 1789 was the first revolution started by the Jews to set up this new world order under a one world government. This uprising was the French Revolution headed by Weishapts Illuminaty. The entire revolution was conducted by a pack of Jewish leckies who went under the name of Jacobins. It was these bushrats that came up with the [blank space circled by Keegstra] to butcher innocent people with. This revolution was far from bloodless. The Jacobins would ride around in packs and bash in childrens heads, rape the women and then drown them. They would also cut open the stomachs of men and let them bleed to death. This by the way was all done to follow Weishapts first point in his plan. To destroy the Monarchy in France. The Jewish problem also plagued Russia for some time now. This problem was evident in Russia since the time of Catherine the Great.

Catherine the Great was known, for some unknown reason to me as the enlightenment. She made a fatal mistake of allowing [illegible] of German Jewish intellectuals into Russia. These Jews wanted to destroy the monarchy and bring in the new world order by means of a bloody revolution. They started strikes, riots propaganda, tried to get control of the monetary system. They even try sabotage and assasination. This attempt under Catherine was not very successful.

After Catherine the Great, Alexander was appointed Czar. He wanted to make life for the Surfs (slaves) more enjoyable. The nobles of the country were extremely opposed to this idea so they supported the new Jewish evil groups which had now entered and set up shop in Russia. Alexander I refused to get involved with these Jews.

Alexander I first son Constantine refused to take the throne because of these ruthless jewish groups so his brother Nicholas I took the crown. The Jewish Zionist groups of Russia saw this as a great excuse to get a revolution started and overthrow the monarchy. They started spreading a filthy lie that Constantine wanted a constitution limiting the power of the Czar and Nicholas did not feel this was proper so he had overthrown Constantine and was going to be a ruthless ruler. The surfs of Russia believed these sweet talking Jews and began to revolt. Nicholas I heard about the rebellion against his monarchy and sent his troops in to prevent further advancement of this revolution. His troops were successful and Nicholas I put on severe restrictions on the Jewish revolutionary leaders. Nicholas I then announced he would put through a constitution. His attempt failed because of Kazzar Jews assasinating high government officials in charge of this constitution. Nicholas I became reactionary and formed a private Government Police which was to shut down all secret societies. He also set up consentration camps in Siberia for these political prisoners. Because of

Nicholas I's cruel treatment of these Jews anti-Semitism was formed. Nicholas I's name was smeared all over Europe.

In the years 1851-56 Nicholas got involved in a bloody engagement with the English. The confrontation was known as the Crimean war. This was started because the Russians went down to liberate the Moslems from the Jews who were harassing the Moslems. The Jews spread the word that the Russians were going down to invade Palistine. This land belonged to the English so they went down to protect their land.

After Nicholas in 1885 a liberal, Alexander II was crowned Czar of Russia. Alexander II wanted reforms so in 1860 he got the immancipation of the surfs through. In 1881 he was finally [Keegstra writes, "ready to"] set up a constitutional monarchy for the first time in Russia. This was after 9 attempts on his life. After a funeral for one of his counterparts Alexander II stopped off to review the guard. It was here that the fiendish Jew Sofie and her accomplisses threw a bomb attempting to kill Alexander II. Alexander II however was not hit, but while attending the wounded a second bomb was thrown. This was the end of Alexander II and his constitutional monarchy.

After Alexander II's death his sone Alexander III was put on the throne. He had Sofie and her gang tried for the death of his father. All six were executed at the same time. (let it be known that Lenin's the first dictator of Russia brother was one of the six). Alexander III also chased approximately 800,000 Jews out of Russia. It was now that official Zionism comes to be known to the world led by a Jew named Herzel.

In 1894, another Czar was crowned in Russia. He wanted Russia to catch up to the rest of the world in productivity. Doing this he relaxed his hold on the Jewish Zionist groups. He ran into problems because of this so he started to get rid of the Socialists and started to return Russia to Christianity. New agricultural ideas and interest free loans brought in industry. Now in productivity Russia outdid the United States of America. This progress lasted until 1917 when the Revolutionary thugs led by two Jews Lenin and Trotsky started a revolution and overthrew Nicholases government. When this revolution was over the Czar and his family were dead. This was Russia's last Czar. Since the Revolution, Russia has been under the control of several Jewish Zionist Communist leaders backed by the International Bankers (Jews). Under these leaders life in Russia is like living in a dump. For the last 64 years they have had poor weather (this is since the Revolution) and therefore have had 64 crop failures. This is not because of weather but because of the communist power in charge.

The First World War was started by the Jewish Zionist groups to destroy England [Keegstra adds "and Russia"]. England found at this time was the only European country that the Zionist groups didn't really have a hold on. The war was also to create debt throughout the world so that the International Bankers (Jews) could take advantage of the bad situation the world would be in. It was also started so that Lenin and Trotsky would have an easier time in overthrowing the

Russian Monarchy and setting up a communist state. By the end of this war most of what the Jews had planned was complete.

The Second World War was to finish off what the First World War didn't complete. It was also so that communist Russia could pick up more real estate in Europe. After World War II approximately ½ of Europe that was free before the war was now under communist rule.

This essay shows how the Jews are conspiring to take over the world. And when they do they will set up a New World Order under a one world government. I have shown in this essay since 1776 with Adam Weishapts five point plan the Jews have been causing anarchy and chaos throughout the world. I have also shown that where ever the communists rule it was set up by the Jews. In my opinion this must come to a dead halt. We must get rid of every Jew in existence so we may live in peace and freedom.

Keegstra gave Denis a grade of 65 per cent on the essay. It was, after all, a good reflection of what had been taught in class. It certainly contained no research from "garbage" sources. Such sources might have told Denis the Crimean War began in 1853 and that, at the time, Palestine was a province of the Turkish Empire. From the notes and essays, it is clear that Keegstra took a rather reckless attitude towards dates accepted in conventional texts as well as towards more mundane matters. One essay explains that Shakespeare's the *Merchant of Venice* was banned in the United States because of its anti-Semitic portrayal of Shylock. Another essay says Napoleon Bonaparte was "wiped out" at the Battle of Leipzig in 1815. (Napoleon lost in Leipzig in 1813, but ended his imperial career after Waterloo, in 1815.) Another student had the Franco-Prussian War of 1870 fought in 1868. None of the incorrect dates or spelling errors (Bulcan for Balkan, Auto von Bismarck for Otto von Bismark, aurator for orator) were corrected by Keegstra. The important thing was to lay the blame for war, famine, pestilence and disaster on the Jews.

It went on for years. The students, like many of their peers, didn't talk much to their parents about school. They liked Keegstra and if his ideas were novel, they were also unchallenged. There were no Jews in Eckville for the students to compare with the dark and shadowy caricatures sketched in social studies class.

Danny Desrosiers, the track star, was to recall later: "If you trust a teacher, and believe what they say and you're enjoying the class, you have less of a reason not to believe what they say."

It wasn't as though Keegstra forced people to accept his beliefs. Some students did; some ignored him. In the end, though, they all had to write their papers the right way.

But there was a hitch. Paul Maddox, then 14, talked to his mother, Susan, about Keegstra's teachings. She was amazed, then upset, then angry. "Paul was being indoctrinated, not educated."

Other parents were concerned as well. Sherron Wolney, another of the three valedictorians, said her parents were not happy with what was being taught.

Susan Maddox complained about Keegstra. He had been warned a year before to stop teaching the conspiracy theory as fact, but he had ignored the caution. On December 8, 1982, Keegstra was not in class. He was never to be in class again.

# 2
# Defiance

---

*Mine enemies chased me sore, like a bird without cause.
They have cut off my life in a dungeon and cast a stone
upon me.*

—Lamentations 3:53-54

---

Eckville is off the beaten track. The highway from Red Deer, a half-hour drive east, rolls past the turnoff on towards Rocky Mountain House. Eckville is about five kilometres off the highway, settled in the rolling parkland which, to the west, is displaced by the Rocky Mountain foothills.

The government sign announces Eckville's population as 700, about 100 shy of the actual total. Further on, the town has erected its own greeting: "Welcome to Eckville, a nice community to live in."

There's nothing to distinguish Eckville's low-slung skyline from that of any other western Canadian rural town. The grain elevators and water tower telegraph Eckville's location to travellers. The wide main street of storefronts opens quickly into a polyglot of older frame houses and postwar bungalows.

The economic recession of the early 1980s hurt the town. Eckville survives on the business of area farmers and the oil companies that explore central Alberta's still-attractive oil-and-gas fields. With the energy slump the drillers went away and so did the lucrative jobs for strong young men who used to find

*Eckville's main street, looking southeast. The school where Keegstra taught is about two blocks north. (Canadian Press photo)*

summer work on seismic crews or well-paying jobs after graduation on the rigs. Several stores on the main street are empty. The school was on the main street, just up from Art Carritt's service station. Eckville's young, especially those who didn't farm, often left to build lives in Red Deer, Calgary or Edmonton. The slump increased the exodus.

That wasn't the case when Jim Keegstra came to Eckville. Alberta was on the edge of an unprecedented 10-year oil and gas boom. Although he was a newcomer, he was hardly an outsider. Born and raised in central and southern Alberta, he understood small-town life, rural values.

The school was having one of its chronic staff shortages. Keegstra, the new teacher, despite a relative lack of experience in academic subjects, quickly won respect because of his ability to hold students' interest in class and act as a Christian role model in and out of school.

Yes, there were complaints. Keegstra, a zealous anti-communist, sneered at two farm families who bought Soviet-made Belarus tractors. They were doing nothing but supporting a slave state, he believed. Undaunted, the sons of the two farmers drove the offending machines past Keegstra's house in an impromptu parade.

Then there was the matter of his apparent attitude towards Roman Catholics. Keegstra taught about the influence of the Catholic Church, especially in the medieval period. He spoke pejoratively about the corrupt practice of selling indulgences and the political power of the Church, the Inquisition and the role of the Jesuits. Catholics in the class felt intimidated. It wasn't so much what he said, because for the most part it was historical fact, but the way he said it. They got the distinct impression he was challenging their faith. So did their parents and a series of complaints flowed into the superintendent's office during the 1970s. After a group of parents wrote then-superintendent Frank Flanagan a letter, Keegstra was told to tone down the material on Catholics. Flanagan told the parents Keegstra had taken the warning to heart.

The experience left Keegstra with the suspicion that a group of parents in the town was scrutinizing his every utterance in social studies class. It was a conspiracy of sorts. The goal: to get rid of the man whose teachings they found unacceptable. Membership in this coterie of meddlers would soon grow.

Late in 1981, the father of David Ackerman, a student in Keegstra's Grade 12 social studies class, took exception to an essay David was assigned to write on the historical role of Judaism. He contacted trustee Kevin McIntee, who in turn called Robert David, who had succeeded Flanagan as district school superintendent in 1979. David, a large, fierce-looking man with an air of authority, soon heard from Ackerman directly and paid a visit to the Eckville school December 18.

In a meeting with Keegstra and school principal Edwin Olsen, who was there mainly as an observer, David explained the complaint and asked for a copy of the essay. Keegstra replied he had left Ackerman's paper at home, where he did his marking, but offered him the essay of another student, Danny Desrosiers, who wrote on the same topic. Here, in part, is what Desrosiers wrote:

Judaism is a religious cult which claims to trace its origins to Abraham. But most Jews in the world today are Jews by religion. This mixture makes the Jews very dangerous. The Jew today follows the writings of the Talmud. The Talmud is a set of ancient rules set down by many of the scribes and Pharisees from before Christ's era. This Talmud teaches the Jews to hate Christ. They call the Christians goyim [dog] and say that the Christians are cursed. But Christ said the Jew was a curse and would be a curse to all nations they were allowed into.

The Jews believe that by the year 2000 they will control the world. They are going to do this through welfare states and bloody revolutions. They want to set up their "New World Order" with the headquarters in Israel. . . .

The Jews are the controlling heads behind all Communist and Socialist governments in the world today. They either have direct involvement in the policymaking or they support the government with money. They are planning to get all the governments grouped into one world dictatorship. They are doing this through groups like the United Nations, NATO and the Warsaw Pact. These groups are so large that they are easily infiltrated and controlled by the Jews. . . .

As you can see, the Jews are truly a formidable sect. They work through deception and false [illegible word] to achieve their ends. They are very powerful and must be put in their place.

David, shocked by what he had read in the essay and in some students' notes, told Keegstra he found the material alarming. He wanted to investigate further and Keegstra offered him the names of three students, whom David interviewed with Olsen present. The superintendent had, at the beginning, assumed that the material in the notes and essay had come from outside the class or that the students had made it up. But the interviews confirmed Keegstra had taught it to the students and they had accepted it as factual. Only one of the three told David the material was ever debated in class.

David told Keegstra the course appeared totally one-sided, but Keegstra insisted the social studies text, though not used in class, was available to students to present the other side.

The interview became heated. David was upset by the assertions the Holocaust was a hoax. Keegstra suggested David had been duped by the Zionists into believing the Holocaust had happened, just as the conspiracy manipulated all historical accounts to suit itself. David had gone into Eckville puzzled and left understanding it was Keegstra who was the source of the material.

He told Keegstra he would send him an official letter directing him to stop teaching the conspiracy as if it were fact. Keegstra stuck to his guns, stubbornly insisting he had not strayed outside the curriculum guidelines. The volatile David warned that if Keegstra didn't comply with the directive the matter would be brought before the Lacombe County Board of Education.

Keegstra saw it as the start of a personal vendetta. David now was lumped with the conspirators out to get him fired.

David sent his letter December 18, the day of the interviews. Keegstra was teaching his ideas about the conspiracy in a vigorous, forceful and persuasive manner and the students were accepting them as fact, the letter said. It was the first in a series of epistles on the issue as Keegstra held out for more specific proof he had violated the guidelines of the broadly outlined curriculum. In January, David sent Keegstra another letter advising him he would be fired if he didn't comply with the directive. The following month, Keegstra appeared at a board meeting to explain himself and, he claimed, won support of the members for his teaching approach.

"They all said, 'Why isn't this history taught? Why is this history censored?' "

Nevertheless, Keegstra received another letter dated March 9, essentially reinforcing David's initial directive and asking for written assurance Keegstra would comply. Keegstra replied he would continue to follow the curriculum guide as he had done in the past. The two sides simply were talking past each other. Students would testify later that Keegstra told them about the confrontation with school authorities and its outcome, but paid only lip service to the directive.

"I assumed the letter just said to carry on the way I was going," Keegstra said later.

But this storm would not blow over as the others had done.

The following October, Susan Maddox, a British-born, part-time nurse who had married a local farmer, chanced to look at the Grade 9 social studies notebook of her son, Paul. Here's what she read:

THE BANK OF ENGLAND—Banks operate on the creation of credit. Credit is the creation of numbers in a ledger. A ledger is a sheet of paper with columns on it, one called the credit column, another the debt column and another the balance column. The credit they create is theirs. In other words bankers own all the money they create and when loaned out is eventually wanted back. However, there is a severe problem. The banker wants more back than he created. This is called interest or usury. Therefore a debt is established which must continue to grow because it can never be paid back. A man or nation in debt eventually must become slaves. Only the bankers have the power to create money. Therefore eventually we must become their slaves. The bankers knew they could create all the money and charge usury. Then eventually all countries and their people would be under their control. That's why bankers support socialism.

In the midst of a passage on the roots of capitalism and the industrial revolution appeared this passage:

In England and Europe there existed a secret society whose ambition and goal was to destroy Christian civilization and establish One World Government under a New World Order. These evil [word missing] saw in the Industrial Revolution with its upheavals an opportunity to spread their evil religion in the robes of legitimate reforms such as medicare, pensions, secret ballad [ballot] U.E.I. [Unemployment insurance]. To put the plan into motion the first thing they needed was control of the creation of credit—money. Because all these reforms required money and only source of money would be these evil men, eventually all nations would be slave to them.

And finally:

*THE PLAN OF THE SECRET SOCIETY*—Illuminati (Commies) The plan for one world government was hatched about 570 B.C. by those we call today Judaists. This group almost died out in the 7th century AD. But in 740 AD a kingdom called the Khazars—their race was Mongols, Turks and a few Finns—adopted the Judaic religion. These people today are called the Jewish Zionists. These people also have as a goal One World Government and a new world order.

The notes went on to list the Illuminati's master plan to take over by destroying legitimate governments, corrupting society's morals and spreading secular humanism and evolution. It would use terror, deception and promises of equality for women to foster its plans.

Motto of Socialism—Illuminism and Communism—the good and happiness of man. This motto has been used effectively to have people build their own jailhouse through the use of majority vote. Through the control of the press, publishing and money, votes could be bought easily.

Paul's notes ended there because Mrs. Maddox pulled her son out of class and wrote a letter to Robert David. She wanted Keegstra out of social studies.

On December 7, which Keegstra later noted sardonically was the anniversary of the Japanese attack on Pearl Harbor, the Lacombe school board held a five-hour meeting, voting 11-2 to terminate Keegstra's contract immediately. The grounds: failure to follow the board's previous directive about teaching the conspiracy theory. He would not set foot in a classroom again.

The firing made headlines. About 94 students at the high school, roughly half the enrolment, signed a petition asking that Keegstra be reinstated. Only about 20 of his former students refused to sign.

Townspeople were similarly surprised by the dismissal. Their mayor was a respected member of the community. The firing was seen as unjust, an infringement of Keegstra's right to express himself.

Opinion in the high school's staff room mirrored that of the town. Teachers saw the firing as a threat to their flexibility and the Alberta Teachers' Association, which had gone to bat for Keegstra during his wrangles with the school board, protested the firing as an over-reaction.

Keegstra launched an appeal of the dismissal, which was heard in Edmonton over four days, beginning March 22, 1983, by Madam Justice Elizabeth McFadyen of the Alberta Court of Queen's Bench, who was sitting as a Board of Reference. Keegstra testified frankly about his views and the judge heard from other parties to the dispute.

Three weeks later, McFadyen ruled the firing was valid, that Keegstra had been fairly dismissed because he had not followed the curriculum.

The teachers' association, which had felt uneasy about its perceived obligation to defend a member teacher, said it would not appeal the decision. Later, after its own investigation, the association would recommend the Department of Education lift Keegstra's teaching certificate, in effect making him unemployable as a teacher in the province.

Keegstra, who meanwhile had returned to his former profession and was fixing cars out of a rented garage in nearby Bentley, dubbed the appeal hearing a kangaroo court controlled by the conspiracy. Noting the presence at the hearing of observers from various Jewish groups, Keegstra decided something was up.

The Jews used the news media to embark on a big smear campaign against him, he said. The case presented by his lawyer should have won the appeal hands down, but the outcome was pre-ordained, said Keegstra.

Despite publicly stated qualms about the outcome of the hearing by Keith Harrison, the teachers' association executive assistant for members' services, Keegstra said the group was riddled with Zionists who had set him up. The conspiracy then succeeded in intimidating the association's discipline committee into investigating the case itself and recommending his teaching certificate be suspended, Keegstra thought.

Jewish groups were, indeed, concerned by what they saw as a lukewarm condemnation of what Keegstra stood for, both by his own profession and Alberta's leadership in general. Herb Katz, head of the Edmonton Jewish Community Council's community relations committee, took the lead in expressing the feelings of the 5,000-member Edmonton Jewish community. The city's Jews were at first shocked, then baffled, by the Keegstra affair.

Alan Shefman, national director of field services for the League for Human Rights of B'nai B'rith Canada, said the Alberta Jewish community—about equally divided between Edmonton and Calgary—had been complacent about anti-Semitism. But the Keegstra affair brought the community together. Shefman recalled attending a meeting at Edmonton's Jewish Community Centre. The building was jammed with 1,200 people, more than twice its 500-person capacity. Many had not been to a community gathering in years.

What spurred this outburst was not simply Keegstra's teachings, but an event that took place almost before the ink was dry on McFadyen's appeal ruling. It would change the complexion of the whole affair.

On April 19, the *Edmonton Journal* published an interview with Stephen Stiles, a provincial government member of the legislative assembly from the riding of Olds-Didsbury, in central Alberta. The government backbencher, who holds university degrees in commerce and law, said he was not personally aware of any evidence that millions of Jews were massacred by the Nazis. The comment exploded like a bomb on the Alberta political landscape. Stiles, rebuked by Attorney General Neil Crawford, apologized a few days later in the legislature, saying he was sorry he had upset people with his views. But he did not retract them. Alberta's Jews were not appeased and called for Stiles's expulsion from the Progressive Conservative party caucus. Crawford said he felt Stiles's apology closed the matter.

About a week later, the rest of Canada, which had been following the Keegstra affair mainly through newspaper wire service reports, got a first-hand look at the man himself. The Canadian Broadcasting Corporation's television newsmagazine *The Journal* introduced viewers to Keegstra and to a number of his former students, most of whom seemed satisfied with Keegstra's explanations about the way the world worked. The story now would not fully leave the public eye until after the trial.

The case of the anti-Semitic teacher had developed into a full-blown controversy. Jewish groups accused politicians of insensitivity; parents, teachers and the education department battled over who was responsible for Keegstra's long tenure at Eckville High; churches suffered recriminations over Keegstra's self-professed Christianity. Even Keegstra's own political party, Social Credit, was irreparably harmed by its connection to the affair. The party's Alberta wing first fired, then reinstated, Keegstra to an executive position. National Social Credit leader Martin Hattersley resigned in protest, saying he did not want to be associated with a party that was being thought of as the successor to the Nazi party. The following year, after Keegstra had been charged with wilful hate promotion, he would run unsuccessfully as Social Credit candidate in the September 4 federal election. He lost his deposit.

Alberta Premier Peter Lougheed, who had kept silent publicly about the Keegstra affair, finally made a statement May 12. Rising in the legislature, Lougheed pleaded for racial and religious tolerance.

Lougheed did not refer directly to Keegstra, but assured Albertans that there was no resurgence of bigotry and prejudice in the province. Still, he said, this didn't minimize the gravity of the matter.

"History shows that elements of bigotry such as the anti-Semitism in this recent case can grow like a cancer if not challenged and vigorously condemned by those in positions of responsibility," he said.

Lougheed sketched the outlines of a policy to combat racism, including an education program in the schools conducted by the Alberta Human Rights Commission, and an investigation into how tolerance for minorities could be fostered in the school system. The government would soon announce the formation of the Committee for Tolerance and Understanding, headed by former Conservative member of the legislature Ron Ghitter, a Calgary lawyer who was, himself, a Jew. The committee would hold extensive hearings around the province before issuing a report 18 months later.

The publicity surrounding the Keegstra case naturally cast a spotlight on the town he presided over as mayor. Discomfited by residents' qualified displays of sympathy for Keegstra, many Canadians concluded the people of Eckville accepted his views. It seemed they were not prepared to disown the man because of one facet of his character. The town came to be identified with the man. One resident remembered chatting with two women at a roadside coffee shop in British Columbia. They recoiled in suspicion when he mentioned he was from Eckville.

Outsiders tried on their own to counter what they saw as the former teacher's influence on the town. Alberta Jews politely rejected an offer by Mel Lastman, the Jewish mayor of the Toronto suburb of North York, to come to Eckville and speak to its citizens. However, one young Jewish man did come to town and set up shop on the main street sidewalk with a sign inviting passers-by to come and talk to a Jew. He had few takers.

More effective was a documentary shown at the school on the Holocaust and a visit by three survivors of the Nazi concentration camps, whose accounts made students weep. But others were seen by reporters later laughing and joking about what they had heard. Calgarian Jack Downey sponsored an essay-writing contest for the school's students. The two winners received a two-week trip to West Germany, which included a tour of the Dachau concentration camp. Both were moved by what they saw but one said he still thought Keegstra had been an excellent teacher who should have been allowed to stay on and teach something other than social studies.

The counter-offensive against Keegstra's teachings only served to reinforce some people's opinions about the conspiracy.

"This is the time the Jewish conspiracy group wants to build some sympathy," said Danny Desrosiers.

In spite of such views, Keegstra was coming under fire on his home turf. A group of citizens led by the Eckville Chamber of Commerce and the Royal Canadian Legion, asked Keegstra to resign as mayor for the good of the town. Town councillor George Schmidt said Eckville had been represented across Canada "as a haven for narrow-minded bigots and rednecks. . . . Mayor Keegstra, you're doing a great disservice to your community, your province and Canada."

But Keegstra refused, saying the media and the conspiracy had been working to smear him and the town. Council backed him in a 4-2 vote. Councillor Robert Kraft, who had voted for the mayor, said he believed 90 per cent of the town still supported Keegstra and laid blame for Eckville's notoriety at the feet of Keegstra's detractors.

Keegstra, who said frequently through his trial he considered Lord Acton's dictum, power corrupts and absolute power corrupts absolutely, as words to live by, tried to pass a resolution through town council asking the local Presbyterian minister to leave town and go back to the Maritimes. Keegstra had taken exception to Rev. Kenneth Macleod's critical comments about Keegstra's views, published in the *Calgary Herald*.

In early June Keegstra was presented with a petition signed by 240 of Eckville's 375 eligible voters calling for his resignation. Sixty-two other voters signed a second petition asking him to stay on. Keegstra hinted he thought the first petition might have been a fake, and the issue was shelved. Still, organizers hoped they had sent a message to the outside indicating two-thirds of the town disagreed with what Keegstra believed.

But Keegstra's stonewalling had bought him only a little time. Five months later, on October 17, 1983, Keegstra lost the only real race he had run for the mayor's chair to the man he replaced due to illness in 1978. Joe Leach outpolled Keegstra 278 to 123 in an election that saw 92 per cent of the eligible voters cast ballots. Only one of the councillors who supported Keegstra's fight against resignation the previous spring—Jim Lecerf—was re-elected, placing last among the six candidates who would take seats on the council. Marg Andrew, the woman who led the 1978 complaint about Keegstra's teaching, also won a seat, garnering the fourth-highest vote total.

Keegstra said the town had been completely swayed by media hysteria, desperately seeking to take the spotlight off Eckville by turfing out the main irritant. Reporters had descended on the town like a pack of vultures, he said, and at least 20 turned out on election night to record his downfall.

Keegstra was now a discredited teacher and a defeated politician, presumably consigned once more to make a living fixing automobiles. But the wheels were already in motion that would keep the magnifying glass on Eckville and its best-known citizen for another year.

# 3

# The Truth Shall Set
# You Free

---

*Behold, I have given him for a witness to the people.*

—Isaiah 55:4

---

It is a rural face. Not a farmer's face, weathered and lined, but a small-town face, canny and sharp-featured. The deep-set, pale blue eyes set off a long, straight nose, the reference point jutting under a pair of light-sensitive, tinted, wire-frame glasses. The hair has gradually turned an iron grey with streaks of silver.

At rest, Jim Keegstra's face can look stern, but when he begins talking the smiles come easily. His ideas animate the mouth, the brow and, behind the tinted lenses, the eyes.

"I wouldn't have minded being a farmer," says Keegstra, relaxing in an easy chair in the living room of his clean but cluttered mobile home.

The house, which the family bought in 1980, rests in a small trailer park near Eckville's showplace community centre, a few blocks from the junior and senior high school where Keegstra taught for more than 14 years. There are grandchildren's toys scattered on the carpet. Family and religious pictures adorn the walls and side tables. The four children, two girls and two boys, are grown, but not far away. Larry, the eldest son, is pastor of the fundamentalist Diamond Valley Full Gospel Church, which Keegstra attends.

Jim Keegstra was born in Vulcan, south of Calgary, not far from the Kirkcaldy-area farm his parents helped work. He arrived in 1935 along with a twin brother, John, six years after his parents emigrated to Canada from Holland. The family, which ultimately included seven children, moved around the province while Jim's father, Klaas, hired out to other farmers. In 1948, Klaas Keegstra could finally afford his own place near Alhambra, west of Eckville.

The family settled. Keegstra took his high school at Rocky Mountain House and travelled to Calgary for an auto mechanic's ticket at the Southern Alberta Institute of Technology. He worked at the trade from 1954 until 1961, when Ross Ford, brother of Keegstra's boss and a pioneer in developing Alberta's vocational education program, persuaded him to become an automotive shop teacher. He took a two-year diploma course at the University of Alberta teacher's college in Calgary, graduating in 1963. For the next four years he took summer courses to obtain his Bachelor of Education degree.

With his wife Lorraine, a Crossfield, Alberta native whom he married in 1956, Keegstra moved around central and southern Alberta on teaching assignments—industrial arts at Cremona's junior high school, automotives at a high school in Red Deer and a variety of courses at a Christian school in Medicine Hat—before arriving in Eckville in 1968.

Keegstra left the Medicine Hat Christian School under something of a cloud. At his trial, Keegstra said he resigned from the small, privately run school because of a disagreement over theology. Keegstra had been teaching his amillennialist interpretation of the Bible, which disputes accepted interpretations of the apocalyptic end recounted in Revelation, in the boys' Sunday School class. The school's resident theologians took offence, he said, but they couldn't refute his arguments.

"All they did was start getting mad at me, hating me," he said. "The minute you come up with a different idea and a different point of view, you're in trouble."

Rev. Alvin Maetche, president of the school and now a Methodist minister in Fergus Falls, Minnesota, said Keegstra's strong, opinionated personality led to a mutual parting.

"He was actually a very effective teacher," said Maetche. "But he was very difficult to work with. He couldn't get along with the faculty and administration. He also wasn't happy with the discipline procedure we followed. He was after more strict discipline."

Keegstra got a chance to indulge his desire for strict discipline at Eckville, a rural school with the traditional approach to the

*Jim Keegstra in a pensive mood. (Canadian Press photo)*

matter. He became an enthusiastic disciple of the rod—or in his case the pointer and yardstick. One former student recalls Keegstra earned the nickname "the pointer prince." Admittedly, many of the school's teachers liked to use the pointer to keep rambunctious country boys in line. One even tossed a student over several desks like a sack of fertilizer. But for Keegstra, the pointer seemed to be an extension of his arm. Students were whacked for sticking their feet out from under desks, whacked for talking, whacked for giving incorrect answers and whacked for sassing the teacher. Keegstra wouldn't abide disrespect.

He preferred, as well, to solve his disciplinary problems at the classroom level, without a trip to the principal's office. Randy Forhan remembers his short stint in Keegstra's social studies class in 1968. A self-confessed rowdy, Forhan was talking to a classmate when he said Keegstra struck him on the face, breaking the pointer in the process.

"I stood up," Forhan recalled. "I was thinking of drifting him and he told me to take my books, get out and never come back."

He didn't, and his father didn't discover the fact until two weeks later. Keegstra had not bothered to inform the principal. Tom Forhan, Eckville's druggist, went in to see the principal, not to complain about the blow—"I'm a little bit of a disciplinarian myself"—but to demand an explanation of why he had to learn by accident that Randy had been kicked out of class.

"He [the principal] didn't know anything about it," said the elder Forhan. "I thought that was pretty weird and I let him have it with both barrels. I thought he should be running a better school than that."

Keegstra's penchant for corporal punishment landed him in court on an assault charge in 1971. Kevin Baker, a 15-year-old Grade 9 student, returned home one January day with three red welts on his back, inflicted by Keegstra during a social studies class. The teacher had spotted Baker reading a book during class.

"He told me to put the book back or he would show me how hard he could hit," Baker testified at the trial before a provincial magistrate.

Baker threw the book on the floor and Keegstra struck him several times.

"I've found the pointer to be very effective," Keegstra testified. "I've never used it in abuse. I'd rap students on the fingers if they weren't working or tap them on the side of the leg to remind them to keep their feet out of the aisle, or on the head or neck to stop them from daydreaming."

The judge acquitted Keegstra, saying the beating had been a reasonable use of the teacher's authority because Baker had defied him.

Former students say those who got a licking from Keegstra generally deserved it. But sometimes not.

Terry Safron recalled he went curling with his father one night and, spying Keegstra a few sheets away, flashed him the double thumbs-up sign popularized by the character Fonzie in the television comedy *Happy Days*. Keegstra apparently took it the wrong way. The next morning, the teacher grabbed young Safron in the hallway and "got physical."

"He said if I ever did that to him again he'd tune me in but good," Safron said.

But it wasn't Keegstra's attitude towards discipline that upset some Eckville parents. It was what he was teaching their children.

Keegstra's philosophy developed with measured progression, intertwining his Dutch Calvinist Christian roots with die-hard Social Credit ideology, based on the purist interpretation of the movement's founder, C. H. Douglas—staunch anti-communism and a reflexive animosity towards big business, big government and entrenched institutions in general. By the mid-1970s it had melded into an all-encompassing world view rooted in Christ's biblical condemnation of the Pharisees, the pervasive influence of the Jews in society and the unalterable belief that Judaism is a force for evil in the world.

Keegstra's skepticism was inherited from his devoutly religious parents. He recalled his mother listening to a radio program about the partition of Palestine in 1948 and commenting there was no biblical justification for the state of Israel.

"A lot of evangelicals said it was the fulfilment of prophecy," said Keegstra. "I remember once my mother saying, 'This is so anti-Scripture I can't listen to this any more,' and so she turned off her radio."

Reformed Calvinism is founded firmly in Scripture, Keegstra said. It rejects the concept of the Jews as the Chosen People as a Jewish fable. Jews are atheists because they rejected Christ as Savior, Keegstra learned from his mother.

"A Jew hates Christ. That's the key thing that got me thinking."

Keegstra believes the emphasis on millennialism and deciphering the end times prophecied in Revelation dates from the 1800s, when the conspiracy began tampering with biblical scholarship. It is the conspiracy that has pushed the concept of the Jews as God's Chosen People, when in reality those who accept Christ are the Chosen, he said. It is the conspirators who foster the belief that the return of the Jews to Palestine signifies that the "last days" are near, when the Messiah will return to Earth for the 1,000-year reign of peace—the millennium.

"Christians are going to be taken out and the Jewish people are going to enrol in this millennium," says Keegstra.

There will be a Judgment Day, according to Keegstra, but the millennium will not be a tangible thing.

"The Kingdom of God is not meat and drink," he said. "The

Kingdom of God is within a person. The Kingdom of God directs how you think and, therefore, how you act."

Keegstra's distrust deepened at university when in one of his education courses, he received a mark of 35 per cent for an essay on juvenile delinquency which he said displeased his professor. Keegstra said his Christian approach to the problem differed from the instructor's secular humanism.

"He says, 'You've got a completely different world view than I have and I don't like it,' " Keegstra recalled.

Keegstra soon discovered if he wanted to pass the course he would have to play the game. He would write what the professors wanted to hear, then insert his own arguments to make his point.

It wasn't until the late 1960s that Keegstra began tying things together. As a teacher in rural schools he was required to handle not only his specialty, industrial arts, but also teach academic courses, such as science and social studies.

As he researched lesson plans for the two social studies courses he was assigned at Eckville, he came to the conclusion that the secular humanists had control of the curriculum. The textbooks left gaps in their explanations of how historical events occurred and what proofs they did offer were extremely weak.

Keegstra discovered Nesta Webster, an English writer who, in the 1920s, produced several books of political history with conspiracy and subversion as central themes. Keegstra, noting endorsements from prominent authors such as Winston Churchill, historian Arnold Toynbee and H. G. Wells on the jacket covers, read Webster's works with interest.

Through Webster he learned the outlines of a worldwide conspiracy based on "kabbalistic Talmudism" led by atheistical Jews whose goal was one world government and a new world order. Conventional historical works were censored by this Hidden Hand, which controlled major institutions such as government, the banks and the media. Although Webster's works had been around for decades, no professor dared use them and she had become discredited over the years, Keegstra said.

"The minute you start accusing men who call themselves Zionist Jews of subversive and perverted actions you are in trouble. You have no right to accuse them, according to this Hidden Hand which controls everything."

Keegstra found other works which buttressed Webster. Through his Social Credit acquaintances he learned about the Canadian League of Rights, operated out of Flesherton, Ontario, by Ron Gostick, whose mother had been a member of the legislative assembly in the Alberta Social Credit governments of William Aberhart and his successor, Ernest Manning. The League had a monthly newsletter called the Canadian Intelligence Service which, said Keegstra, told the real story behind news events and gave insights into history even before they came out in books. He became a subscriber.

Keegstra's political activism took two courses. He was a perennial Social Credit candidate, losing first provincially in the 1971 landslide which swept the Social Credit out of power after 36 years and replaced them with Peter Lougheed's Progressive Conservatives. After that, his disaffection from mainline Social Credit deepened and he became more closely identified with the Douglasite faction, which adhered to the founder's economic policies more strictly.

Douglas, a British engineer turned economist, railed against what he saw as a world financial system controlled by Jews which used debt to enslave people. In 1939 he wrote to Hitler: "The Jew . . . is the parasite upon and corruption of every civilization in which he has obtained power."

Douglas advocated the government develop a form of "social credit" paying each citizen a monthly dividend out of government coffers which could be put back into the economy to create activity. The inflationary aspects aside, when the Aberhart government tried to implement such a plan—which was to include a drastic restructuring of debts—in the mid-1930s, it was quickly struck down as unconstitutional. The special dividend scrip the government printed was ridiculed as "funny money" and the party quickly shifted to conventional fiscal conservatism, which helped keep it in power through nine elections.

Keegstra ran unsuccessfully for federal seats, but did better in local government. After being elected to Eckville's town council, Keegstra assumed the job of mayor in 1978 after Mayor Harold (Joe) Leach was forced from the post by ill health. Keegstra won the job on his own in 1981 by acclamation and stayed on, despite demands from Eckville residents that he resign, until the 1983 election, when he was defeated.

In 1974, Keegstra suffered a serious heart attack which kept him away from teaching during much of the year. He still takes medicine to regulate his heart.

Meanwhile, the classroom teachings which would get Keegstra into trouble had begun to crystalize. Reading molded Keegstra's initial, vaguely understood notions about a conspiracy into a complex belief system that explained most major historical events and current political and economic developments.

Students soon came to learn how the world worked according to Jim Keegstra and how it could be set right by exposing the Jewish conspiracy theory and implementing the original master plan of C. H. Douglas.

These teachings were all within the curriculum as Keegstra understood it, and until his dismissal he would challenge school officials to show him where he departed from it. Under existing social studies policy, teachers are at liberty to inject what they consider relevant material into the class to spur discussion and thinking among students. The curriculum document contained only broad topic outlines and the later course guide, prepared by a committee of teachers, did not rule out any of the material he used, Keegstra maintained.

Jews didn't play much of a role in the early years, when Keegstra stressed the evil of communism and the historical power of the Roman Catholic Church. No one was uncomfortable with his anti-communism, but the tone of his historical teachings about Catholicism upset some of the community's Catholic parents, who complained as early as 1974. But it wasn't until Marg Andrew and several other parents actually wrote a letter of complaint in 1978 that Keegstra received his first official warning to tone down. Frank Flanagan, school superintendent for the Lacombe County Board of Education at the time, had a long meeting with Keegstra. Reports of the outcome differ. One student claimed he overheard Flanagan read the riot act to Keegstra, but both Keegstra and Flanagan say the meeting was cordial and businesslike.

"He was a man of strong opinions who expressed his opinions strongly," Flanagan, now an Alberta Education Department consultant, said recently.

Keegstra said Flanagan read the students' notes and found nothing to quarrel with. The material had a historical base.

Flanagan, himself a Catholic, would play down the matter with parents and later to the police, saying it was better ignored.

"It was age-old tripe that I'd heard about Catholics many times."

Keegstra told his students they were expected to know the textbook version of events for the departmental examinations, which were abolished after 1973, but he made sure they got his theory as well. The information his pupils gleaned in class often found its way to other teachers, but Keegstra said he didn't meet any serious opposition from his colleagues. Anyway, the proof was in the pudding, he suggested. His students, for the most part, had done well. Some had even gone on to university.

So the gulf grew wider. The concerned parents felt placated by the superintendent's assurances the problem had been handled. Keegstra believed he had been vindicated by Flanagan's inability to exact a recanting of his teachings. Flanagan seemed to feel Keegstra understood the warning. A few weeks later, it was business as usual.

# 4

# Maintiens le Droit

*What is history but a fable agreed upon?*

—Napoleon

As a maelstrom of controversy swirled around the Keegstra affair, the Attorney General's Department ordered transcripts of the Board of Reference hearing.

Attorney General Neil Crawford said in April he seriously doubted there would be any grounds to bring a criminal charge against Keegstra. By July, a review of the transcripts had produced the opposite conclusion.

A six-member RCMP investigation team, led by Cpl. Barry Kutryk of the General Investigation Section, fanned out across Alberta, interviewing some 300 witnesses, 220 of them former students. Kutryk, later promoted to sergeant, had a reputation for methodical investigations. He decided to go back five years into Keegstra's teaching career. It was a manageable period of time when former colleagues and students might be expected to have some recollections of what they had seen and had been taught. Detectives found the vast majority of former students recalled what Keegstra taught about Jews.

From the beginning, investigators sought written evidence such as notes and essays, material similar to that which had offended Paul Maddox's mother. Most former students did not have any notes; others had only a smattering of their school material. The notes and essays became the main criteria in judging the value of students as possible witnesses. Their personal recollections became secondary, no matter how strongly they now felt about what they had been taught. Nor did the prosecutors look for evidence of hatred of Jews in the students. In fact, one student admitted hating Jews, but was rejected as a Crown witness because he had no notes.

Many students sympathized with their former teacher and even those who didn't considered him a good instructor, Kutryk, a 15-year veteran of the force, said later. "There were very, very few that showed any obvious animosity towards the man. I can't think of any actually."

Not surprisingly, the students wondered aloud whether what they told the police would get Keegstra into trouble. Kutryk said he was non-committal.

"We didn't know whether there would be any charges," he said. "I stressed to the students I couldn't say where my investigation would go."

Kutryk's team interviewed teachers, getting little more than opinion accounts of Keegstra based on staff-room discussions of his theories. School Board Superintendent Robert David and his predecessor, Frank Flanagan, were also interviewed but, said Kutryk, the best evidence boiled down to what was in the notes and essays.

During the first week of August, Kutryk and Constable Dirk De Jong visited Keegstra's home, armed with a warrant to seize any of his library that might be relevant to the investigation. The interview lasted more than eight hours and Kutryk remembers Keegstra being congenial and talkative, displaying no animosity towards the police or anyone else. "He was kind of a nice type of fellow, that was my first impression," said Kutryk.

Keegstra, who had been out helping a friend bring in hay from his field, remembered the two investigators were polite and cordial.

"They were typical, I would say, of the security service, Mossad [Israeli secret service], KGB type," he said.

Keegstra brought out the boxes of books the policemen were after and said later they were surprised at what the books contained. They seized 58 in all, including some which Keegstra felt weren't relevant, such as a few on predestination.

According to Keegstra, the two investigators seemed sympathetic after the interview, expressing surprise Keegstra hadn't been violent or abusive, as they had been led to believe.

"They were looking for a criminal that wasn't there," he recalled one of them saying. "They said this would never get to court. I said, 'You've got to be kidding.' "

Kutryk had no recollection of that part of the conversation.

By late fall of 1983 the results of the investigation were in the hands of the Attorney General's Department. Under the hate

*Former school teacher Jim Keegstra sits in the living room of his Eckville mobile home. Some of the books he says helped convince him of a Jewish conspiracy are at his feet. (Red Deer* Advocate *photo)*

promotion statute Crawford would have to personally authorize the prosecution. It could not have arisen from a citizen's complaint. A lot was already publicly known about the details of the case because of the Board of Reference hearing.

"As I recall the process, there was enough known about the case that we knew we had to consider charges under this section," Crawford said.

Still, a public conception that Keegstra had done something wrong was not enough to sustain a prosecution; the material evidence must be there. Crawford considered the decision on whether to proceed the most difficult he had to face in his first six years as attorney general.

Legal opinions from department officers spurred the investigation, but, aware of the difficulty in proving a charge under the hate promotion law, Crawford wanted the endorsement from the lawyer who might ultimately have to prosecute the case: Bruce Fraser.

"We wanted to say, 'This is what you have by way of evidence,'" said Crawford. "'Suppose you as general counsel might take this to court. Suppose there are all the challenges that are present in a trial. Do you think that based on the evidence you can sustain it?'"

Fraser took a fairly short period of time over the New Year to review it, and said yes.

"It wasn't a long answer," Crawford recalled. "It wasn't on the one hand this, on the other hand that. He said he could try the case and look to a conviction."

"I could see that a lot of other things needed to be done, in terms of fine-tuning the case," Fraser said. "But it was basically all there."

Jim Keegstra was indicted January 11, 1983, under Section 281.2(2) of the Criminal Code of Canada on a charge of wilfully promoting hatred against an identifiable group, to wit the Jewish people.

# 5
# A Clear and
# Present Danger?

*We must not make a scarecrow of the law, setting it up to fear the birds of prey.*

—William Shakespeare, *Measure for Measure*

Ernst Zundel argued that the systematic destruction of European Jewry by the Nazis never happened; that it was a hoax perpetrated to inflict guilt on western civilization and help promote the founding of the state of Israel as a place of refuge. Jim Keegstra taught that an ancient, worldwide cabal of Jews has manipulated history for hundreds of years, twisting the lives and fortunes of people and nations to its own nebulous ends. Both men rejected arguments to the contrary. Both closed their ears to the accounts of eyewitnesses to the Holocaust. Both gleaned tidbits of information to fit their murky jigsaw puzzles and "prove" their theories. Keegstra, especially, never seemed to use the logical principle that states the simplest answer to a question is most likely the correct answer. He preferred, rather, to reject the simple answer, that historical calamities were caused by accepted, conventional factors, in favor of his tangled and convoluted "international Jewish conspiracy."

But are these dark and somehow pitiful ideas deserving of criminal prosecution? Laws against the promotion of hatred are an exercise in social compromise. They are an attempt to balance the rights of free expression against the rights of minorities to be free from the cruel slanders of hate-mongers and rabble-rousers. The Keegstra and Zundel trials focused attention on the sections of the Criminal Code of Canada dealing with hate promotion and the publishing of false news likely to cause social or racial intolerance. The argument falls between those who see free speech and free expression as sacred rights to be tampered with only at the peril of democracy, and those who call for protection of minorities otherwise left without recourse against slurs, slanders and libels.

The law under which Zundel was convicted dates back to the 1890s, but the anti-hate law under which Keegstra was charged and convicted is much more recent. It was the product of a federal committee appointed in 1965 to study the phenomenon of hate literature and its promotion in Canada. It was led by Maxwell Cohen, then the distinguished dean of the law school at McGill University in Montreal. One of its six members was a law professor from the University of Montreal, Pierre Trudeau, later to be Canada's prime minister. The committee studied examples of hate literature then in circulation. Much of it was virulently anti-Jewish.

In its final report, the Cohen committee called for an anti-hate law. "We act irresponsibly if we ignore the way in which emotion can drive reason from the field," the report said. It argued that the community has both a right and a duty to protect itself from what the committee called "the corrosive effects of propaganda."

The bill that would add Section 281 to the Criminal Code prompted an acrimonious debate in the Canadian Parliament in the late 1960s. The discussion pitted those who felt the statute was a dangerous step down a slippery slope towards greater government curbs on free expression against those who felt it was part of the state's duty to protect those members of society who were the victims of hate-mongers.

Since its passage, the debate has gone on in sporadic fashion. There are those who say the law should be strengthened; who say it is a toothless statute almost impossible to use. They would remove the word "wilfully" from the law, saying the requirement to prove intent shackles prosecutors. The need to prove intent could allow hate-mongers to escape the law because demonstrating lack of intent is a defence, even if the actual effect of their actions was the promotion of hatred.

Some also contend that the requirement that the provincial attorney general give formal approval to the laying of a charge should be removed. In most cases in Canadian law, a policeman or an ordinary citizen with a reasonable belief that an offence has been committed may lay a charge. In some statutes, though, the attorney general's formal consent is required. In the Zundel case, for example, no such consent was required, but it was needed to charge Keegstra.

Neil Crawford, Alberta's attorney general at the time of the Keegstra prosecution, gave his consent to the charge. He said he valued the provision that keeps the attorney general, a province's chief law officer, involved in such proceedings. "I think the philosophy behind requiring the attorney general's consent is that you don't want ... to have warring factions among small, perhaps racial groups, seeing that charges are laid against other groups all the time."

Crawford admitted that finding the proper balance between free expression and the protection of minorities is a task fraught with pitfalls. He said his ideas changed even in the period in which Keegstra was being tried.

"Now maybe the incitement to hatred is sufficient [grounds] to take away a person's freedom of expression, but I'm less sure of that than I was and that's an evolution in thought," he said. Although Crawford and his officials laid the charge against Keegstra, the soft-spoken politician said his philosophy on the question of free speech is not set in stone.

"Although my thinking has changed, I find it one of the most difficult judgments to try and make as to where to draw the line.

"I'm not so sure that we can have total freedom of expression, but I weigh very heavily in favor of freedom of expression."

The general Canadian point of view about the hate laws seems to be that such limited prohibitions pose no real threat to freedom of expression; that some limitations must be expected. As Alan Borovoy, general counsel for the Canadian Civil Liberties Association, says: "The issue is not whether you choose order or liberty, but how much of each you choose. You cannot have liberty without order, you cannot enjoy order without liberty." He believes Canadians, as a society, have long tended to extend their trust to government, whether or not government has demonstrated itself worthy.

That attitude, coupled with a Canadian tendency to value "peace, order and good government" over the looser, more libertarian attitudes of their American neighbors, may be a factor in the passage of laws such as Section 281. As June Callwood says in her book, *Portrait of Canada:* "[Canadians] trust the government and police to act in the best interests of society even when they [the government and police] do not seem to be doing so. They trust that authority knows best."

The contrasts with the United States are stark. In the U.S., the First Amendment to the Constitution enjoins Congress from making any law abridging freedom of speech, and the courts have tended, in this century at least, to take that prohibition literally. In 1919, Mr. Justice Oliver Wendell Holmes wrote a dissenting opinion in the case of Abrams vs. U.S. The defendant and four others were convicted for distributing leaflets attacking the United States and its First World War Allies for intervening in Russia against the Bolsheviks. Their appeal to the Supreme Court of the United States was rejected but Holmes, in a dissent from the decision supported by Mr. Justice Louis D. Brandeis, argued against upholding the conviction and cited the First Amendment: "We should be eternally vigilant against attempts to check the expression of opinions that we loathe and believe to be fraught with death unless they so imminently threaten immediate interference with the lawful and pressing purpose of the law that an immediate check is required to save the country." This judgment, reduced in legal shorthand to the doctrine of "a clear and present danger," was to become a major test of the limitations on free speech and expression.

Other U.S. justices have offered absolutist views on the subject of First Amendment protections for free expression. Mr. Justice Hugo Black, long noted as a man who took the Constitution literally as it was written, said in 1967: "I believe the federal government is without any power whatever under the Constitution to put any type of burden on speech and expression of ideas of any kind (as distinguished from conduct)." Mr. Justice William O. Douglas, also writing in 1967, said: "The First Amendment allows all ideas to be expressed—whether orthodox, popular, off-beat or repulsive. I do not think it permissible to draw lines between the 'good' and the 'bad' and be true to the constitutional mandate to leave all ideas alone."

While it must be admitted that the United States Supreme Court has, at times, lost sight of these principles—particularly during the McCarthy years of the 1950s—it has generally held that free expression—however repugnant the ideas expressed—is a right to be trifled with only at great hazard to liberty and only when the very fabric of the Republic is at stake.

In Canada, though, ideas and attitudes differ. Even the new Charter of Rights, which contains many of the sentiments expressed in the American Bill of Rights, begins with the language of compromise. The preamble to the charter says the rights it contains may be abridged by such limits as are deemed "reasonable" in a free and democratic society. Borovoy, in a 1984 paper prepared for the conference of the Canadian Institute for the Administration of Justice, points out a number of areas where Canada imposes limitations on the freedom of expression. "In democracies like Canada, the problem with encroachments on freedom of expression is not a wholesale invasion; it's a piecemeal erosion. The danger here is that an accumulation of legislative enactments and judicial pronouncements will serve, not to eradicate, but to emasculate freedom of expression."

He notes that Canadian courts have restricted picket lines, calling them a form of collective action rather than a means of expression. He outlines a case where a student was jailed for 10 days for writing in a university publication that a certain trial was a mockery of justice. The crime? Scandalizing the courts by bringing the court and the trial into "public hatred, contempt and ridicule."

On the present anti-hate laws, Borovoy stands opposed. "I could see no objection to a law which purported to prohibit the incitement of racial violence in situations where there was an imminent peril that the violence would occur," he says. "But 'hatred' is a much more nebulous and therefore dangerous concept."

He notes that in 1975, police in Toronto cited the anti-hate law in arresting some young people who were distributing leaflets that said, "Yankee Go Home." The charges were eventually dropped, but the potential for misuse was there.

He cites another case where well-meant laws might have been bent to a purpose for which they were not intended. In the 1940s, the government of Maurice Duplessis in Quebec tangled with the Jehovah's Witnesses. The Witnesses, who felt the Roman Catholic Church was behind Duplessis, responded with anti-Catholic literature and were charged with seditious libel. The Supreme Court of Canada dismissed the charges, holding that "the mere creation of inter-group ill-will will not sustain a charge of sedition." Borovoy's fear, though, is that in a similar case, the creation of such ill-will might sustain a charge of promotion of hatred.

In the two decades or so that the anti-hate law has been on the books there have been at least three convictions. One was an unreported Winnipeg case in which a guilty plea was accepted in a plea bargain. There was a conviction in Ontario in 1977, which was overturned on appeal. There was the Keegstra case.

In the 1977 incident—Regina vs. Buzzanga and Durocher—two men, Robert Buzzanga and Jean Wilfred Durocher, were charged for distributing a handbill entitled "Wake Up Canadians, Your Future is at Stake." The pamphlet was produced in the midst of a controversy in the Essex County area of southwestern Ontario over attempts by the francophone minority to persuade the local school board to build a French-language high school. There was a great deal of local opposition to building the school and the tension rose after the school board elections, which produced a majority of members opposed to the school. At that point, Buzzanga and Durocher—who were both French-Canadians—produced their handbill. Among other things, the publication said: "You are subsidizing separatism whether it is in Quebec or Essex County"; and "The British solved this problem once before with the Acadians, what are we waiting for?"

The accused testified they believed that prejudice, rather than financial problems, was the reason behind the opposition to the new school. They said their pamphlet was meant as a satire which would demonstrate the prejudice against French-Canadians. They hoped to create an uproar and force the provincial government to intervene. Judge J. P. McMahon, sitting without a jury, convicted the two men under Section 281. He held that "wilful" as contained in the law, meant "intentional as opposed to accidental." The judge said the two men admitted they intended to cause controversy, furor and an uproar. Buzzanga and Durocher were sentenced to two years' probation.

The case was appealed to the Ontario Court of Appeal and was heard by a panel of three justices. The main item at issue was the trial judge's definition of the word "wilful."

The appeal court's decision held that "an intention to create controversy, furor and an uproar is not the same thing as an intention to promote hatred and it was an error to equate them." The convictions were set aside and a new trial was ordered. The Crown, however, did not follow up and the matter died.

It was with this background that Crawford and his officials in the Alberta Attorney General's Department approached the issue of Keegstra and his teachings. They studied the meagre precedents and the circumstances of the case. They considered the existence of the students' notebooks and the situation (the idea of a teacher's authority in the classroom).

In the end, despite some doubts about the principle of the law, a consensus of opinion held that the case against Keegstra was winnable. That, said Crawford, was the key. Although there was public concern, the decision was made on the basis of legal considerations. "We look for the ingredients of the offence and do our very, very best . . . in ignoring the amount of public agitation that may be present," he said.

"It doesn't even matter whether we think it's a good law or a bad law, because my view of my duty is that I take the criminal law as I find it."

# 6

# The Legacy of Hatred

---

*My God will cast them away; because they did not heark-
en to them; and they shall be wanderers among the
nations.*

—Hosea 9:17

---

Anti-Semitism is a term coined by Wilhelm Barr, a German
author of anti-Jewish tracts, in his 1879 book, *The Victory of
Judaism over Germanism.* It was generally thought the word
gave hatred a higher tone, a pseudo-intellectual veneer for
venom. Whatever the terms of reference, the phenomenon of
Jew-hatred goes back more than 20 centuries. It has spared no
Western country, and no era, displaying remarkable endurance.
Fear of witches has died out. Belief in magic potions is rare, but
anti-Semitism, despite its baggage of disrepute, survives.

The Jews, who have never made up a major portion of the
population of any European country, have been stigmatized for
centuries. They have been persecuted out of all proportion to
any influence they might possibly have had. They have been
condemned as Christ-killers, children of Satan, heathens and
infidels. They have been accused of sacrilege and ritual murders.

Christian churches have long led these persecutions, most
drawing their anger from a line in the Gospel of John, chapter
eight, verse 44, in which Christ speaks to the Jews: "Ye are of
your father the Devil and the lusts of your father, ye will do."

From this shred of Scripture and from a number of other sometimes cryptic biblical references has come a legacy of hatred, myriad killings, tortures, expulsions, robberies and segregations. Jews have been the subject of forced conversions by the Holy Inquisition. During the Crusades, the knights and soldiers who marched across Europe to free the Holy Land from the Saracens often paused in their travels to kill hundreds of Jews. They argued it was silly to travel hundreds of miles to kill infidels when there were unbelievers in their midst.

Most conventional history books and encyclopedias chronicle the extent of persecutions against the Jews, which ran unchecked in Europe for centuries.

During the Crusades, the Jews of Germany's Rhine Valley suffered especially. During the First Crusade, in 1096, hundreds of Jews were massacred in Worms, Mainz and Cologne. Estimates have put the total number of Jewish dead at between 10,000 and 20,000.

In the aftermath of the Crusades came the first of what were to become known as the blood libels. This was the name given to accusations of ritual murder laid against the Jews. They were accused again and again in different places over the years of murdering Christian children and draining their blood to use in exotic and mysterious rites celebrating the Jewish festival of Passover. As recently as this century, such claims were made against Jews, despite repeated efforts over the years by various popes and secular leaders to label the charges groundless. From the Middle Ages on, hundreds of Jews were executed for these mythical murders, often after "trials" in which torture was used to extract "confessions."

Jewish books and philosophies were also condemned. The Talmud, a multi-volume Jewish work with no real equivalent in Christianity, was often a target of persecutors. The Talmud is a collection of commentaries and explanations of Jewish law compiled by scholars in Palestine and Babylonia between the fourth century before Christ and the 10th century A.D. It is both a repository of Jewish oral law and a blend of philosophy, logic and interpretations that lies at the centre of Judaism. The study of the Torah, the first five books of the Old Testament, is embodied in the contents of the Talmud.

The very existence of the Talmud was seen as a threat by Christendom for centuries and it was itself the subject of persecution. The idea presumably was that if the knowledge and philosophy were destroyed, the Jews themselves would be destroyed as well. In 1240, for instance, King Louis IX of France actually ordered the Talmud itself, the very words, put on trial in Paris on a charge of heresy. In a predictable outcome, the Talmud was condemned for defaming the Christian faith and sentenced to be burned. Between 1242 and 1248, 27 wagon-loads of Jewish books were burned in Paris. In 1267, Emperor Frederick II ordered all Talmudic works and Jewish prayerbooks in Italy seized. In 1559, 12,000 volumes of the Talmud were burned in Cremona, Italy. In Poland, in 1761, there was another orgy of book-burning after a Jesuit published a book which "proved" the Jews guilty of ritual murder charges.

From the time of the Crusades, through the Reformation of the 16th century, Jews in Europe were randomly persecuted. They were accused of responsibility for the Black Death, the bubonic plague of the 14th century. It was said the Jews spread the plague by poisoning wells, even though they themselves also died of the disease. They were expelled from various countries, re-admitted, then thrown out again, usually with little more of their worldly goods than they could carry on their backs. There were outbreaks of savage violence, sometimes spontaneous, sometimes at the urging of fanatic churchmen. The Inquisition raised high the pyres in Spain and Portugal, reserving special horrors for Jews who converted to Christianity and then returned to Judaism. To this day, Spanish descendants of converted Jews, known as Marranos, are an ostracized group in some areas.

The Reformation appeared to hold out some hope for the Jews because, in the beginning, Martin Luther called for better treatment for the Jews and condemned the persecutions visited upon them by the Church. However, it soon became clear that Luther's idea was that kind treatment would win the Jews over to Christianity by showing them the error of their ways.

When they remained steadfast in their faith, Luther's forebearance turned to bitter anger. He published several strongly anti-Jewish books in the 1540s, just before his death. He urged the burning of synagogues, accused the Jews of acting as spies for the Turks—then the major threat to Christian Europe—and said Jews should be expelled from Christendom.

Jews had settled in eastern Europe about the time of the Crusades, when they were driven from central Europe on the blades of the Crusaders' swords. Their lot in Lithuania and Poland was little better than in the rest of Europe. Like their brothers elsewhere they faced blood libels, expulsions and persecutions. They also found a new word, *pogrom*—Russian for devastation. It came to mean an attack on the Jews. Jewish homes and synagogues were burned, men killed and women raped in hundreds of pogroms during the next nine centuries.

Over the years, the Jews were forced to be roamers and exiles. In 1290, they were expelled from England. Early in the following century they were driven out of France. In the 1490s, Spain and Portugal purged themselves of their Jewish populations.

Left without roots or homelands, without access to land ownership or membership in the guilds of workmen which controlled manufacturing in pre-industrial Europe, the Jews turned to other livelihoods. While Christian Europe generally heeded the biblical injunction against usury, it was not thought to apply to the Jews, so they became moneylenders. That brought down slurs and anger on their heads from debtors. They also became travelling merchants, a trade that produced more slurs that still exist in our language today.

The *Oxford English Dictionary* records the verb "to jew," meaning "cheat, bargain with (person) to lower his price." The entry is noted as both derogatory and colloquial.

Emancipation for the Jews and the beginning of the end of widespread, institutionalized anti-Semitism probably dates back to the late 18th century and the American and French revolutions. In the original American 13 colonies, there had never been any great anti-Semitism. Archives preserve cordial letters between George Washington and the Jewish communities of several cities. In France, the revolutionary doctrine of Liberté, Egalité, Fraternité helped spark passage of a bill of rights for Jews in France, granting them, in theory at least, equality.

The twentieth century, while it brought about a general easing of anti-Semitism in its later years, also brought the single most devastating attack on Jewry every contemplated or carried out—the Holocaust.

Despite the work of so-called revisionist historians, there is no doubt that the Nazis systematically murdered millions of Jews in a carefully planned campaign of extermination. Any library will contain dozens of fully documented accounts of the Second World War destruction of European Jewry. Deeper research will uncover the massive documentation assembled for the war crimes trials at Nuremberg. Auschwitz, Treblinka, Chelmno, Maidenek and Belsen existed and were used to slaughter millions. There are still eyewitnesses alive to testify to the workings of the death camps and the crimes against humanity carried out in the name of making Europe *Judenrein* —free of Jews.

In Canada, as in other countries, anti-Semitism is an inescapable fact, although it has never reached the excesses found in some other countries. In the 19th century in Canada, Jews

*Jews being rounded up during the destruction of the Warsaw Jewish ghetto in 1943. Keegstra's students were taught the Nazis created the ghetto to protect the city's Jews from the Poles. (AP photo)*

found themselves subjected to the same sorts of racial slurs that were attached to other groups of ethnic immigrants. Newspaper editorials complained about Jewish immigration as they had earlier condemned the influx of Irish and would later decry the arrival of Chinese, Japanese and Italians.

In the 20th century, there were anti-Jewish, fascist movements in both Ontario and Quebec before the Second World War, although these died out when the war broke out with Germany. The high point of anti-Jewish sentiment may have been reached in the immediate pre-war years with the refusal by Mackenzie King's Liberal government to accept desperate Jewish refugees fleeing Hitler's Germany. In the phrase current at the time, "None is too many."

There were other examples as well. In Alberta the Social Credit government, which held power between 1935 and 1971, had an early anti-Semitic streak in it which Premier Ernest Manning fought to stamp out. Much Canadian anti-Semitism today is of the keep-the-Jews-out-of-the-country-club variety, although there are people who still feel uncomfortable around Jews and there are those in some circles who tacitly maintain anti-Semitic sentiments and try to keep institutions narrowly

*Rows of dead prisoners at the destroyed Nordhausen concentration camp near Leipzig, Germany, at the end of the Second World War. Keegstra said the Holocaust was a hoax created by the Jews to gain sympathy. Most of the deaths in camps were due to starvation, disease and bombing in the last weeks of the war, he believed. (Canadian Press photo)*

WASP. There have also been incidents of violence, vandalism and desecration. Synagogues have been streaked with swastikas, Jewish graveyards have been vandalized and Jews have been beaten or verbally abused. In 1983, the League for Human Rights for B'nai B'rith reported 48 anti-Semitic incidents—down from 63 the previous year. The cases involved attacks against Jewish property and institutions, as well as harassment of individuals. Ontario and Quebec, which contain about 80 per cent of Canada's Jews, accounted for 46 of the 48 episodes. The actual magnitude of Canadian anti-Semitism is hard to gauge accurately because the league says it believes that for every incident documented, five go unreported.

Today, anti-Semitism seems to be changing. It no longer comes solely as an isolated act of a single person or sect. North America is seeing a widespread network of anti-Semitic propagandists and agitators. Books such as *The Hoax of the Twentieth Century*, which claims the Holocaust was a fraud, and other works that twist widely accepted historical records and resurrect old slanders are produced and distributed by revisionist publishers throughout North America. The Institute for Historical Review in California produces anti-Semitic material, as does the Canadian Intelligence Service of Flesherton, Ontario.

The so-called revisionist historians who produce much of this anti-Semitic material, particularly works which question the Holocaust, have no formal training in the field. Arthur Butz, author of *Hoax of the Twentieth Century*, is an electrical engineer by training. These "historians" and their "research" fly in the face of conventional history and accepted academic findings, though they rarely have the credentials to back them up.

Keegstra himself has the same problem, in that he was trained as a teacher of industrial arts and auto mechanics, but found himself teaching social studies. Staff shortages mean many teachers end up "doubling in brass" in a field outside their specialty. In the field of historical research, this same kind of thing has led to much of the revisionism published today.

Some of the revisionists have actually revived one of the hoariest bits of anti-Semitic propaganda, the "Protocols of the Learned Elders of Zion." This document, purporting to be the minutes of a meeting of Jewish conspirators discussing their timetable for world domination, was discredited just after the First World War.

It was shown to be a forgery, the work of the secret police of Czarist Russia, by a British journalist in 1921. It was shown that a major portion of the "Protocols" was lifted, almost intact, from a French satire against Napoleon III. Other passages were plagiarized from various fictional sources. Yet the bogus document is still held up by some as proof positive of the Jewish conspiracy.

It has had a remarkable longevity, despite its lack of bona fides. In the 1920s, the "Protocols" were reprinted in Henry Ford's newspaper, the Dearborn (Michigan) *Independent*. There were reprints in Nazi Germany and several Arab countries have published it in recent years. The Kuwait Ministry of Post and Telephones actually sent copies to postmasters general around the world, urging them to display the book in post offices. Hitler used the "Protocols" as a source in *Mein Kampf*.

The reasons for anti-Semitism, however obvious they may seem to its practitioners, are more obscure to the majority. For one thing, Jews have long been trapped by the illogic of their tormentors. If Jews banded together, either for safety or because they were physically walled away in ghettos, they were taunted as people who thought themselves better than others and condemned for refusing to blend in with other nations. If Jews tried to assimilate, they often found themselves banned from political and social life, prohibited from mixing with others and legally barred from marriage to non-Jews.

Hitler ranted against the Jewish refusal to take a full role in the expanding German nationalism of which he preached. When he took power, though, he passed racial laws to ensure that Jews could not join in the mainstream of German life.

Modern anti-Semitism, as well, may be moving down a different path because of the creation of the state of Israel. Bruce Elman, an Alberta lawyer and a Jew, theorizes that anti-Semitic writings and speeches of today are basically aimed at destroying the legitimacy of Israel and thus undercutting modern-day, North American Jewry. To strike back at Israel, the anti-Semites slash at the two main underpinnings of the Jewish state. Faced with the argument that Israel has a right to exist because it is the ancient, biblical homeland of the Jews promised to them by God, the revisionists trot out the Khazar theory. This concept says today's Jews are not the children of Abraham but are actually descendants of an obscure Turko-Finnish tribe called the Khazars, which converted to Judaism 1,200 years ago. The real Jews of the Bible, inheritors of God's covenant with Abraham, conveniently disappeared over the years, leaving the Khazar-descended imposters behind. These phonies have no right to Palestine, the argument goes, so Israel has no right to exist.

The second argument for Israel's legitimacy holds that it is a place of refuge for those who suffered in the Holocaust and a partial repayment for the destruction of European Jewry. The revisionists attack this by denying any Nazi atrocities. If there were no death camps, then there are no refugees and no need for Israel.

There may be another cause of modern anti-Semitism, this one rooted in history and unconnected to Israel. Looking back to the period following the Crusades and the massacres of Jews by the Crusaders, a curious pattern emerges. It was in the aftermath of the Crusade massacres that the first of the blood libels surfaced. It was almost as if the Jews had to be denied any rights as victims. Instead, lies were concocted to make them criminals. Today, 40 years after the end of the Second World War and the systematic murder of millions, there seem to be new deniers who again refuse to allow the Jews a place as victims. The new lie makes them liars at best and evil, world-conquering manipulators at worst. The lie does not allow for Jewish victims.

# 7

# The Lawyers

---

*A lawyer has no business with the justice or injustice of
the case which he undertakes.*

—Samuel Johnson

---

The two lawyers at centre stage in the Keegstra case—Bruce
Fraser for the Crown and Doug Christie for the defence—could
not have been more different in their attitudes towards the law.

Fraser, who turned 43 during the trial, was born in Toronto
and grew up in Montreal. He graduated from Dalhousie University law school in Halifax and was called to the bar in 1973,
joining the Alberta Attorney General's Department soon after.

By the early 1980s he had become one of Alberta's senior
prosecutors. Perhaps his most publicized case was the conviction of Ted Drabick, the Calgary man who, when faced with the
imminent eviction from his foreclosed home, took two bailiffs
hostage, holding one for almost a week before a complicated
settlement of some of his grievances against the bank were ne-
gotiated. Drabick got five years for forcible confinement.

Fraser took personal pride in nailing what he termed "a dirty
lawyer." Sam Doz was convicted of counselling to commit an
offence when, during a trial, he engineered a switch between a
client accused of impaired driving and an acquaintance of the
accused, making it impossible for the arresting officer to identify him.

Fraser spent 18 months as acting assistant deputy minister in the department, charged with reorganizing the Crown prosecution system and setting up its criminal division. Lawyers believed Fraser was destined for a permanent senior administrative post after acting as the minister's pointman in the needed cleanup.

But Fraser said the posting was considered temporary from the beginning and he returned to Calgary as the department's general counsel, the title he held when he was given the Keegstra case. He was later appointed director of special prosecutions, a role which would allow him to pick and choose which cases his office would undertake.

Fraser had a reputation for thorough case preparation, but the complexity of the Keegstra case meant help would be needed. Enter Larry Phillippe who had, at age 26, been called to the bar only three years earlier. Phillippe's boyish enthusiasm and Huck Finn good looks counterpointed the compact, taciturn Fraser.

After graduating from the University of Alberta law school in

*Prosecution lawyers in the Jim Keegstra trial Bruce Fraser (right) and Larry Phillippe discuss a point of law in the Crown office at the law courts in Red Deer. (Canadian Press photo)*

1981, Phillippe worked for a private law firm, handling criminal cases before taking a job as Crown prosecutor in the small, western Alberta town of Hinton. He moved to Red Deer in March 1984 and almost immediately Fraser asked him if he would volunteer to assist in the Keegstra case. It was Phillippe who would do much of the research into the foundations for Keegstra's theory, reading the dozens of books and pamphlets Keegstra used. He also developed many of the legal arguments on evidence. Although he examined only a couple of the student witnesses at the trial, Phillippe was an invaluable resource. When questions arose during Fraser's examinations and cross-examinations, Phillippe could invariably dip into one of the ever-present cardboard cartons and come up with a file or book or transcript which would answer it.

Doug Christie, 39, cut an altogether different figure from his opposite numbers.

Although he graduated from the University of British Columbia law school in 1970, he was, before taking on the Keegstra case, known less for his legal track record than for his political activities. He maintained a small criminal practice in Victoria, B.C., working out of a converted parking attendant's hut across from the courthouse.

Although he earned grudging respect from the Victoria legal community for taking on hopeless-looking cases, Christie's reputation among his colleagues was that of a fringe player.

"I don't think he would deny he's rubbed a lot of people the wrong way," lawyer David Lissom told a reporter after the Zundel case ended. "He's the black sheep of the bar. He marches to a different drummer."

Dermod Owen-Flood, another Victoria lawyer, described Christie as a "hard working, sincere and devoted lawyer. He feels that people have a right to be wrong."

Christie lives in a bachelor apartment in Victoria, but spends weekends at a 12-hectare acreage he owns on the shore of Vancouver Island.

He first sprang to prominence when he formed the Western Canada Concept party, a right-wing, populist movement which espoused separation from the rest of Canada. The tall, intense Christie went on a speaking tour through the West, where alienation against the federal government was at its peak in the wake of the return to power of Pierre Trudeau's Liberals. He found his most receptive audience in Alberta, which soon elected rancher and oil scout Gordon Kesler as the first and only WCC member of the Alberta legislature in a byelection in the central Alberta riding of Olds-Didsbury.

However, the WCC soon fractured under internal feuding, especially over the role of the separatist plank, which even at the height of western anger at Ottawa attracted only one in 10 Albertans and even fewer residents from the rest of western Canada. Kesler was defeated in the next general election.

Christie remained head of the WCC's British Columbia wing, but the party was, for all intents and purposes, moribund by the time the Keegstra affair drew his attention.

Christie's defence of neo-Nazi publisher Ernst Zundel, a case he took on after Zundel learned the lawyer was Keegstra's representative, gave the public a sample of Christie's rough-and-tumble courtroom manner. Christie clashed frequently with Ontario District Court Judge Hugh Locke in what became a seven-week test of wills.

Locke sometimes cut off Christie's interjections and objections with a firm "Sit down!"

"How dare you interrupt a cross-examination in that manner," Locke said angrily after Christie broke into a prosecution line of questioning.

Christie, whose upright stance, round face and blue eyes give him the demeanor of a defiant schoolboy, refused to be cowed by Locke. After Zundel was convicted, Christie hinted he might not be back in court for the pre-sentence submissions.

"Your Honor has no doubt made up his mind as to what is an appropriate sentence," Christie said coldly.

Locke called the "gratuitous insult" uncalled for and ordered Christie to return for pre-sentence arguments, at which time his remarks also would be discussed.

"If I had a dog, I would treat him with more respect than I was treated in that courtroom," Christie would say after the trial. "If that was the way they behaved at Nuremburg, I can understand the result."

In the end, observers believe the case was lost when Zundel took the stand. Under cross-examination he revealed himself as an admirer of Hitler and acknowledged that under a pseudonym he wrote a book entitled *The Hitler We Loved and Why*. It undermined Christie's contention that Zundel was an honest historian researching the truth, a man who had a sincere belief the Holocaust was a hoax. The jury did not accept Christie's summary argument that its verdict would ring through generations, that a conviction would allow politicians to silence opposition by using the law.

Zundel was convicted of the count relating to the Holocaust pamphlet, but acquitted on the charge dealing with a tract on the Jewish conspiracy, about which little evidence had been called. His 15-month jail sentence was appealed.

Christie, worn out and haggard-looking from the Zundel trial, would nevertheless proceed directly to Red Deer to prepare for Keegstra's trial.

Like Fraser and Phillippe, Christie immersed himself in the conspiracy literature which Keegstra used to support his theory, but came to opposite conclusions from the prosecution. There was, he believed, sufficient evidence to raise doubts about the conventional, accepted view of history.

And even if there wasn't, no law should prevent a citizen from believing or professing any ideas, even if they were wrong-headed and unacceptable.

Christie, with his assistant and companion, Keltie Zubko, 31, was ensconced in a rented home in northwest Red Deer which became the headquarters for Keegstra's supporters. As many as 15 people stayed there during the course of the trial, although Keegstra himself commuted daily from Eckville. Christie's living in close quarters with Keegstra supporters paralleled his decision to live with Zundel during that trial.

Christie did little to dispel the question: Does he believe what they believe? Some people answered it for themselves, in the affirmative, and vandalized his tiny Victoria office. Christie said he also received threatening letters.

Whatever conclusions Christie may have drawn after studying the conspiracy theory, it was clear he entered the fight out of a sincere belief that the power of government had set its sights on two underdogs. His comments about the motives of the government in prosecuting Keegstra underscored the evident cynicism he felt towards the system.

His attitude was bound to lead to a clash with the by-the-book approach of Fraser. Despite Mr. Justice John MacKenzie's best efforts to keep the lid on the obvious animosity the two lawyers felt for each other, the tension in the courtroom was often palpable. Feelings manifested themselves more with looks, tone of voice and body language than with actual verbal skirmishes.

Christie, when making an objection, would sometimes stride toward the Crown's table, wheeling abruptly at the last second to return to his place. Fraser, when frustrated, would sometimes drop the traditional "my learned friend," when referring to Christie.

Christie's objections to Crown tactics were often made in a voice dripping with sarcasm, but it was Fraser who perhaps got in the unkindest cut of the trial. Once, when the jury had left for the day, Christie told MacKenzie he had experienced some chest pains and was planning to go to hospital for some tests. If they amounted to anything it could force a delay in the proceedings. MacKenzie acknowledged him, then asked Fraser if he had any comments. The prosecutor, head down, cleaning off his table, murmured, "No chest pains here, m'Lord."

# 8
# The Law

---

*One man's word is no man's word; we should quietly
hear both sides.*

—Goethe

---

If the charge knocked Keegstra off balance, it was only briefly.
He was soon carving out a position on what he saw as high
ground.

"This is not my battle anymore," he told one reporter. "It's
the battle of everyone who loves freedom. Anyone who is
against me is against freedom of speech."

But who would speak for him in court? There were early
indications Keegstra would ask for a government-appointed
lawyer since he said he didn't have the money to hire an attorney. It would have been a surprising move since Keegstra
believed the government was controlled by the very conspiracy
he sought to expose.

However, within a week Keegstra had a champion. After
speaking briefly with Keegstra by telephone, Doug Christie
agreed to take the case in the cause of freedom. For his part,
Keegstra, the Douglasite Social Crediter, found the onetime
western separatist ideologically compatible.

Keegstra's supporters, organized into the loosely knit Christian Defence League, began a fund-raising campaign that
included advertisements in 108 weekly Alberta newspapers.
The amount of donations was never revealed.

Christie was also tight-lipped about his fees, but given his client's resources, the lawyer would have done well to break even over the long court battle. Christie's modest hometown practice stagnated as he worked with Keegstra and with neo-Nazi propagandist Ernst Zundel.

With Keegstra's preliminary hearing set for early June, the prosecution and defence busied themselves preparing their cases. But already there were people questioning the logic of the exercise.

Ron Ghitter, chairman of an Alberta government committee on tolerance and understanding in the school system, essentially put himself onside with the defence, arguing Keegstra's conspiracy beliefs were protected by the Canadian Charter of Rights and Freedoms. Keegstra's views should be tolerated in a democracy, he said. His martyrdom would only generate counter-productive publicity.

Even the woman who effectively put Keegstra in court had second thoughts. Susan Maddox, the part-time nurse who pulled her son Paul out of Keegstra's Grade 9 social studies class more than a year before the charge, said dismissing him from school was punishment enough. Keegstra's firing had initiated a process which resulted in the Alberta Teachers' Association recommending that Minister of Education Dave King suspend his teaching certificate. King followed through in April 1985, two months before the preliminary hearing began. Keegstra was consigned back to the auto mechanic's trade he had left more than 20 years before.

"The charges weren't needed," said Maddox. "It's not going to undo any of the harm that has been done. It will just polarize feelings again."

The hearing opened June 4 in Red Deer to the kind of circus that would reach full flower a year later at the Zundel trial in Toronto.

A trio of Calgary Jews greeted Keegstra and his supporters on the courthouse steps, waving placards denouncing the denial of the Holocaust. Zundel himself, who was attending the hearing to lend Keegstra moral support, organized a counter-demonstration while Keegstra, surrounded by supporters wearing "Freedom of Speech" buttons, pushed his way past reporters into the 60-seat courtroom.

The hearing before Provincial Court Judge Douglas Crowe was originally scheduled to last five days, but stretched to two weeks due mainly to Christie's detailed, often tedious, cross-examinations.

With the attention-grabbing style which would become famil-

*Supporters demonstrate on the steps of the Red Deer courthouse at Keegstra's first court appearance on February 29, 1984. (Canadian Press photo)*

iar in the next year, Christie opened the proceedings by challenging the charge.

"This charge does not allege an offence known to law," he said.

But Crowe, setting the tone for the testy relationship that characterized the hearing, cut him short, saying the charge clearly referred to promoting hatred against an identifiable group—the Jews.

Fraser suggested a publicity ban. In Canadian preliminary hearings, which are held to determine only if sufficient evidence exists to send a case to full trial, bans on publication of the evidence are routine. The idea is to safeguard the impartiality of potential jurors. But Christie, whose option it was to ask for a ban, turned the offer down, saying his client wanted a chance to rebut the distorted image painted of him by the media. The decision was to have significant consequences later.

The Crown called 10 witnesses. Most were former Keegstra

students who attended his social studies classes between September 1978 and December 1982, the period covered by the indictment.

Paul Maddox, then 15, began by reading passages from his class notebooks, written during the six weeks he was in Keegstra's class. The pale, carrot-haired youth told the court Jewish-controlled banks attempted to put individuals and nations into debt slavery. He said Keegstra taught that Jews were responsible for calamities such as the plagues, great fires and famines which befell England in the 1600s.

Faced with Maddox's assertions, Christie developed a style he would use to assail most Crown witnesses during the hearing and subsequent trial. He began probing for holes in the student's memory, trying to open a chasm between Maddox's notes and his recollections.

Maddox's mother, Susan, said on the stand she considered the information in her son's notes biased and inaccurate. Christie pressed her for examples, but she responded that it was all pretty far out and unbalanced.

Rookie teacher Dick Hoeksema, who took over Keegstra's Grade 12 social studies class after the latter was dismissed, testified how the students told him the courts and Hollywood were controlled by Jews and the photographs of Jews massacred in Nazi death camps were products of trick photography.

"One of the first questions I was confronted with was, 'Did I believe in the Jewish conspiracy?' I said I did not."

The notes and testimony gave the public a smattering of Keegstra's topsy-turvy history. Student Lorene Baxter read how Jewish-controlled Jacobins were prime movers in the French Revolution and indulged in what Keegstra called the Feast of Reason. A young Christian virgin was brought to a church, killed and her blood drained over the body of a prostitute. The maiden's corpse was then roasted and eaten, she learned in class.

The court heard that Sigmund Freud, the father of psychoanalysis, was a Jewish drug addict who indulged in sex orgies; that Lenin and Trotsky were rebel Jewish playboys; that Canadian Prime Minister Pierre Trudeau wore a rose in his lapel to signify his membership in the international communist movement; that Henry Kissinger was a KGB agent; and that Winston Churchill sold his soul to the Jews. Franklin D. Roosevelt was under Jewish control during his presidency and committed suicide when the conspiracy informed him he could not become president of the world government it planned, the students were taught.

*Pro- and anti-Keegstra demonstrators became a fixture at Keegstra's preliminary hearing and later the special hearing on the defence's constitutional challenge to the charge. However, at the trial, Justice MacKenzie would ban demonstrators and pamphleteers within two blocks of the courthouse. Here, three Calgary men protest at the preliminary hearing saying they represent the six million Jews who died in Nazi death camps. (Canadian Press photo)*

"Mr. Keegstra told us a lot of stuff written in history books isn't true," said Trudi Roth, who graduated from Keegstra's Grade 12 social studies class in 1979.

Keegstra's teachings seemed to have diametrically opposite effects on different students. Blair Andrew, whose mother complained about Keegstra's anti-Catholic teachings in 1978, recalled everything Keegstra said seemed to have a connection with the Jewish conspiracy, even though there were only 12 direct references to Jews in his notes. The implication came more in class discussions, he said.

"As far as I can determine, he hated the whole race," said Andrew.

CAMROSE LUTHERAN COLLEGE
LIBRARY

But Gwen Matthews testified Keegstra was simply presenting different points of view for the students to discuss, often playing devil's advocate to encourage debate.

"He didn't promote hatred in me," said the fine-featured blond woman. "He didn't force us to believe him."

Christie worried at the students' credibility, suggesting Baxter had missed much in her notetaking and hadn't paid attention in class half the time. The tough questioning brought tears, anger and at times capitulation.

Christie tried to paint Andrew as an actor, enjoying the role of Jew-hater, but the 17-year-old grandson of an IRA fighter became visibly angry at the suggestion.

"I'm ashamed," he said. "I'm not scared to talk about what I was taught."

To the prosecution team, the students' testimony confirmed the feeling it couldn't rely on fallible recollections to prove the charge. The core of the Crown's case remained the notes, essays and tests. Some of the students such as Trudi Roth, when pushed by Christie, simply gave up under cross-examination.

"She just wanted to get off the stand and she was prepared to agree to anything he said," Fraser said later.

And, as had been made obvious from police interviews, some of the students remained personally sympathetic to Keegstra and could be counted on to take the edge off any derogatory testimony if the case came to trial.

Ultimately, some of the most damaging evidence carried the imprimatur of Keegstra himself; essays which students had handed in and which he had marked.

Dana Kreil earned high marks for two essays, on praising Hitler as "one of the most successful people in the world ever to go against the Jews." The other warned of the Jews' "satanic hate" for Christianity. Yet another essay, this one by Richard Denis, concluded: "We must get rid of every Jew in existence so we can live in peace and freedom." The statement went unremarked upon by Keegstra. Denis testified he had suggested eliminating the Jews to please Keegstra, but the teacher had never suggested such a thing in class.

The courtroom remained filled throughout the 10-day hearing, although as the testimony ground on, spectators often snoozed or read magazines. Each morning as they arrived, Keegstra and Christie were greeted by applause or some other demonstration of support. One man, however, threw Keegstra a mocking Nazi salute.

In the end Crowe ordered Keegstra committed for trial, saying he had no doubt Keegstra's statements were capable of promoting hatred. Whether they actually caused hatred in his students was irrelevant, he said, shooting down one of Christie's central arguments. But like his other important points, Christie wouldn't abandon this theme, even as a jury was getting ready to decide Keegstra's fate a year later.

Christie, who had earlier rejected the media ban, complained about distorted news coverage of the hearing.

Having lost the preliminary hearing, Christie was determined the case should never go to trial and applied to have the indictment quashed on grounds that the hate promotion law violated constitutional guarantees to freedom of expression contained in the Charter of Rights.

"Everyone has the following freedoms: freedom of thought, belief, expression, including freedom of the press and other media of communication," says section 2(b) of the Charter.

If the Charter argument was rejected, Christie offered several other grounds for dismissing the case. The Crown hadn't moved quickly enough against the former teacher, which constituted unreasonable delay under the Constitution, and the indictment itself lacked particulars about the specific nature of the offence. The law's constitutionality was also in question because it forced Keegstra to prove himself innocent instead of the Crown proving him guilty beyond a reasonable doubt, Christie argued. Finally, extensive publicity surrounding Keegstra since he was fired almost two years before made it impossible to assemble an impartial jury. The submission came in spite of the fact he had not sought a publication ban during the preliminary hearing.

On October 10, 1984, Keegstra, Christie, his assistant Keltie Zubko and a clutch of supporters walked past the pro- and anti-Keegstra demonstrators, who had become a fixture in the case, into the Red Deer courthouse to make their arguments before Mr. Justice Frank Quigley, a veteran of the Alberta Court of Queen's Bench, the province's main superior court. They were joined by Duncan McKillop, a Turner Valley lawyer who headed the Alberta Bar Association's committee on the Constitution.

Despite the likelihood of two days of dry legal arguments, spectators crowded the 40-seat courtroom in a corner of the building's second floor. Keegstra himself had no place to sit.

"Well, he should certainly have a chair," said the colorful Quigley, directing Keegstra to the prisoner's dock. Eventually, a chair appeared and Keegstra took his place beside McKillop and Christie.

From the beginning, Quigley took an active part in cutting

the defence's arguments down to essentials. He frequently interrupted both lawyers when he felt they were straying or if their arguments weren't having any impact on him.

McKillop handled the constitutional challenge on freedom of expression. Working from a stack of case law, he argued the Charter prohibits unreasonable limitations on freedom and that the onus is on the Crown to prove the hate promotion law is reasonable and justified in a free and democratic society, the proviso contained in the Charter. The silver-haired attorney drew examples of Canadian and U.S. cases involving political and press freedom, as well as religious thought. But Quigley cut him short, saying none of the cases cited had anything to do with hate promotion.

"All those cases deal with something different," said the judge.

But it was Christie who drew the full force of Quigley's ire, by suggesting the proceedings against his client were "an inquisition" and a "show trial," and that the vagueness of the indictment would allow the Crown to submit evidence designed to smear Keegstra's character.

At that, Quigley blew up. Was Christie suggesting an Alberta judge would blithely allow in any old piece of evidence? he demanded.

"You have a duty not to make that kind of suggestion in a legal argument or elsewhere," said Quigley. "If it's not relevant, it will be ruled inadmissible."

Quigley adjourned the hearing briefly, telling Christie to think about what he had said. Moments later the lawyer apologized, saying he didn't mean his remarks to be interpreted as casting aspersions on the court.

Quigley telegraphed his decision on several of Christie's legal points, which he would later confirm in his ruling, especially the issue of publicity.

Christie offered a book of clippings to show Keegstra had been smeared by the press, including a published condemnation from the premier of the province himself, which would surely have an impact on citizen's opinions. Quigley dismissed the argument. People don't believe everything they read in the newspapers or see on television, he said.

Fraser was allowed to make his argument largely undisturbed by Quigley. Freedom, he said, has never been an absolute right in Canada or, for that matter, in other democracies. It has always been subject to limitations. Even if the law was considered restrictive, he was satisfied it would meet the tests for a reasonable limitation as specified by the Charter.

Quigley took almost a month to consider the arguments and spelled out his decision in a 51-page ruling handed down November 5. The defence was shut out on all of its applications.

Quigley adopted almost wholesale the Crown's argument on the limits to freedom allowed under the Charter. Even if the law was submitted to the Charter's test, Quigley said he believed it would pass. Breeding hatred is detrimental to society, causing disruption and destroying the sense of self worth of members of the target group. Limiting the rhetoric was preferable to inflicting serious injury to the community itself and to individual members of the group caught by such prejudice.

"In my view if there is a restriction it is exceedingly slight when compared to the overall right of freedom of expression and particularly when set against the evil or harm that results from hate-mongering."

But Quigley went beyond the freedom of expression argument to point out the Charter specifically entrenches principles of harmony among Canada's diverse minorities as being basic to Canadian values. He cited section 15(1) of the Charter, which wouldn't actually come into force until the following April, which provides "every individual is equal before and under the law and has the right to equal protection without discrimination based on race, national or ethnic origin, color, religion, sex, age or mental or physical desirability." The Charter further requires that its provisions be interpreted in a way which preserves and enhances Canada's multicultural heritage, he said.

Does interpreting the Charter's freedom of expression guarantees to include wilful hate promotion against a group of Canadians identified by race, color, religion or ethnic origin jibe with this direction? Quigley pondered.

"In my view, the only rational answer is no," he wrote.

Quigley quickly dispensed with the other defence applications. There was no evidence of unnecessary delay after the charge was laid and no evidence to support a claim the one-year gap between Keegstra's dismissal from Eckville school and the laying of the charge was due to an ulterior motive by the Crown.

Quigley rejected the argument over negative publicity, saying the defence had tendered no hard evidence other than the clippings that a potential jury would be disposed towards Keegstra's guilt.

He chided Christie for refusing the publication ban at the preliminary hearing.

"Whatever publicity emanated from the preliminary inquiry could have been prevented by the accused," he wrote.

Keegstra's response to Quigley's decision was characteristic.

"Knowing the powers behind it, we knew it would come to trial," he said afterward.

What powers? he was asked.

"You know as well as I do."

# 9
# Justice

*As thou urgest justice, be assur'd; thou shalt have justice, more than thou desir'st.*

—William Shakespeare, The Merchant of Venice

The Red Deer courthouse is a year-old red brick affair. Its tinted windows and low-slung layout give it a bunker-like quality. Inside, though, its skylight and wide foyer lend an institutional airiness. The red ceramic tiles of the floor lead up the stairs to the second storey, which holds most of the courtrooms.

With the raucous Zundel trial over only six weeks before, special precautions were taken for the Keegstra proceedings. In the southeast corner of the courthouse leading to courtroom 201, RCMP constables directed people through an airport-style metal detector. A hand-held wand was used to search those who set off the alarm. Although a sign said purses or briefcases were not allowed into the courtroom, policemen allowed women to carry in their handbags after a brief, but thorough rummage through the contents.

Two pairs of big, varnished doors open into the 110-seat courtroom. A row of white cloth banners hangs from the ceiling like battle flags in an old cathedral. The low-ceilinged, darkly painted spectators' gallery opens into a brightly lit enclosure, giving an impression of looking out from the mouth of a cave into the sunlight. On the left at the front of the room sit 12 chairs in two tiers, seats for the jury. Beside them are a table for the prosecution and the witness box. On the right, the defence table and the prisoner's dock.

In the centre, on a dais above the rest, sat Mr. Justice John MacKenzie. A veteran of the Alberta provincial court, appointed to Court of Queen's Bench (Alberta's superior court) in 1983, MacKenzie faced the most complex case of his 19 years on the bench.

In the red-trimmed black robes of a superior court justice, the jowly, bespectacled MacKenzie appeared a benign, but authoritative father figure. Lawyers who have faced the 53-year-old justice say he runs a tight courtroom, brooking no misbehavior, particularly from counsel. They would be surprised at this MacKenzie, the soul of forebearance at Keegstra's trial, even in the face of the sometimes pushy men at the tables before him.

MacKenzie's first task, as the trial opened April 9, was to rule on an application brought by Christie. The lawyer wanted to examine potential jurors for evidence of partiality. The procedure is rare in Canadian jurisprudence and almost unheard-of in Alberta courts. Presiding in an adjacent smaller courtroom, while the 135 prospective jurors waited next door, MacKenzie listened as Christie argued that publicity surrounding the case for months made selection of an impartial jury nearly impossible. To back his claim, he offered a survey conducted by Gary Botting, a Red Deer College English instructor. Botting had joined the Keegstra entourage after a book he had planned to use in his classes, *The Hoax of the Twentieth Century*, was seized by customs officials at the Canada-United States border. Botting told the judge he "randomly" surveyed more than 400 people at two local shopping centres the previous week and found that just over half were convinced of Keegstra's guilt. Under questioning, Botting admitted he had never conducted a poll before, although he had assisted on some.

Christie also resurrected the defence's book of newspaper clippings. Christie said the book showed his client's reputation had been irreparably besmirched by the media coverage.

Fraser questioned the poll's credibility and said the relationship between the news reports in the clippings collection and the results of the survey had not been made clear.

Most importantly, Fraser said, Christie himself bore some of the blame for the widespread publicity because he did not ask for a ban on publication of evidence at the preliminary hearing. The prosecutor said the effect of news coverage before Keegstra was charged was not relevant, since the issue had not yet come before the courts.

MacKenzie rejected the defence application, concluding that Keegstra was entitled to an impartial jury, not a favorable one. The judge said he found there was not enough evidence to suggest a jury would be anything but impartial. Jurors in Canada are presumed to act on their oath to judge cases on the evidence, he continued.

"I have enough confidence in my fellow Canadians to think they have newspapers sized up, just as they have got other public institutions sized up," the judge said.

Selection of the jury took less than an hour. The courtroom was jammed to standing room only with the prospective jurors, lawyers and court officials. A handful of reporters watched from the doorway as the process began. The names were drawn by lot from a box and the 12 seats filled in short order. Christie quickly used up his allotted challenges and rejected four candidates without cause, which, after MacKenzie's ruling, was all he was allowed to do. The Crown also had four challenges, as well as the option of having up to 20 potential jurors stand aside, to be called again if the original panel was exhausted.

The court clerk went through fewer than 40 names to assemble the final jury of 10 men and two women. It was a young panel, with perhaps two of the men over 40. It was a white collar group—four salesmen, two bankers, a graphic artist, an oil industry worker, an engineering technician, a therapist and a small businessman. One woman was unemployed. They were about equally split between Red Deer and the surrounding rural area, which is included in the judicial district.

MacKenzie's first instructions to the jury took on special significance in light of Christie's preoccupation with publicity. The judge warned the 12 to put out of their minds any previous opinions they may have heard about the case. They were told to avoid media reports on the trial and not to discuss the case with anyone. A verdict must come from a considered weighing of the evidence, without prejudice.

"Prejudice means just what it says, to prejudge," said MacKenzie in his rich baritone. "It's very important you keep an open mind."

Fraser opened his case the next day, but even before the jury filed in, Christie was on his feet in protest. He complained about a leaflet handed out in front of the courthouse the previous day. The pamphlet came from Sigmund Sherwood of Fort Macleod, Alberta, who had stood before the courthouse, dressed in a replica of a concentration camp uniform. The 62-year-old Polish Catholic told bystanders he had been prisoner No. 88 at Auschwitz in 1940. He said he watched trainloads of

Jews arrive at the camp, but said few of the passengers ever joined the inmate population. He quietly handed out his leaflets urging people not to forget the crimes of the Nazi regime.

Christie said he was worried members of the jury might see one of Sherwood's pamphlets and be influenced by its content. MacKenzie agreed and also took notice of a loud, verbal confrontation that had occurred outside the courthouse the day before between Keegstra's supporters and detractors.

In an unusual move, the judge ordered demonstrators to stay at least two blocks away from the courthouse. The building, he said, should be a sanctuary away from the turmoil of public debate. Witnesses, jurors, lawyers and others involved in the trial should be free from intimidation. Legal sources later questioned MacKenzie's jurisdiction in setting the ban so broadly, but no one challenged the action and the placard-waving demonstrators disappeared for the rest of the 15-week trial.

Even so, both sides indulged in some low-key shows of support right inside the courthouse. The regular corps of Keegstra supporters often carried in Bibles and wore lapel buttons with slogans such as "Freedom of Speech" or "Truth—The Final Solution," which included the stylized SS logo sported by Zundel supporters at his trial. Some Jewish spectators, wearing their *yarmulkas*—skull caps—sat amidst the Keegstra contingent. Another man tried to get past security officers holding closed the brightly colored Mexican vest he was wearing. When police stopped him he pulled it open to reveal a large, cardboard Star of David.

Fraser tried a gambit of his own before the trial got underway in earnest. He said Keegstra should be ordered to the prisoner's dock, a bare, spartan bench with high sides and back. Christie said his client, who had been free on his own recognizance for more than a year, was not really a prisoner. As well, the lawyer required that Keegstra sit at the table so they could confer. MacKenzie allowed Keegstra to remain with Christie.

Fraser, facing the jury from behind a tall lectern, now began his outline of the Crown's case. He said the prosecution would attempt to prove Keegstra wilfully promoted hatred against the Jews—a group identified by their practice of Judaism—by communicating statements to his social studies classes between September 1978 and December 1982, when he was fired from Eckville Junior-Senior High School.

Keegstra's beliefs were not on trial, Fraser said.

"It has nothing to do with whether a person can hate. There's no law against that."

Nor did it matter if he succeeded in promoting hatred,

because the crime is wilful, not successful, promotion of hatred. Of course, Fraser said, if the jury found that others acquired hatred from Keegstra's teachings, that would be strong evidence of the promotion.

Fraser said Keegstra laid the blame for almost every historical calamity at the feet of the Jews. They caused the French and Russian revolutions. They started the Civil War to drive the United States into debt. They brought Hitler to power as a puppet and fomented the Second World War to force European Jews to agitate for a homeland in Palestine. But Keegstra told the students Hitler later turned on his benefactors.

The prosecutor said Keegstra taught that the Talmud, the multi-volume assemblage of Jewish law and commentaries, contains a plan to rule the world. The book also allows Jews to kill non-Jews with impunity, Keegstra believed. The teacher spoke of an insidious conspiracy which manipulated nations and peoples in the furtherance of the Jewish bid for world control. Jews were called "money thugs" and "gutter rats" in Keegstra's classroom. They were said simultaneously to control capitalism, socialism and communism and were bent on using these doctrines to destroy the Christian way of life. The prime movers in this great plot were members of a secret society called the Illuminati, according to Keegstra.

"There was almost no major event in world history that was not controlled by the Jews for the purpose of achieving one world government," Fraser said Keegstra's students were taught.

"You are about to be introduced to historical obscurity."

The prosecutor went through Keegstra's catechism of pet beliefs about Jewish influence on history and said they added up to hatred. He asked the jurors to imagine what it was like to be a student, who had probably never met a Jew, and to be exposed to Keegstra's teachings.

"Besides communicating the statements to a captive audience, he made them learn this in order to pass the course. What better way for him to promote hatred?"

Fraser said one would need a video recording to see exactly what went on in the classroom in Eckville. He admitted the memories of former students could not be relied on for an accurate picture of what they were taught up to six years earlier. But the record was there. Preserved in the students' notebooks, essays and test papers was the Crown's main evidence. The students—23 of them—would be called to verify the written material and place it before the jury. While the witnesses would read selected portions, the jurors would get copies of every-thing.

"It is boring, but it's the next best thing to having been there," Fraser told the jury in a careful, measured voice.

He said the Crown planned to call four other witnesses, including the school district superintendent and Dick Hoek-sema, the teacher who took over Keegstra's classes after he was fired. An expert on anti-Semitism would also be called, as would a social psychologist who would discuss the impact of Keegstra's teachings on his students.

Hoeksema was the first Crown witness. He described what he found when he took over Keegstra's 11-member, Grade 12 social studies class. Armed with a history degree and a newly minted teaching certificate, Hoeksema said he was shocked by what he found, or didn't find, in Keegstra's classroom. There were no lesson plans or records, not even a table of student marks from September through December, when Keegstra left.

Hoeksema said his new students had a surprising view of history. The Jews, they told him, controlled everything, from the media to the courts. Hitler was a liberator, a hero, although he went crazy towards the end of the Second World War. One student told the new teacher the world would be a better place had Hitler won the war. Other students said the Jews controlled all publishing and censored all history books. They allowed publication of the Bible, but only Jewish-controlled firms and only when it included a reference to the Jews as the Chosen People. Former Canadian Prime Minister Pierre Trudeau had been placed in power by the international Jewish conspiracy. One student told Hoeksema it would be fine to shoot Trudeau, but he would only be replaced by another puppet.

These ideas surfaced in other classes, Hoeksema said. At first he tried to remain neutral. Later he sought to discourage the discussions.

Grade 9 students, meanwhile, said they felt privileged to know the truth about history. When Hoeksema tried to explain the workings of the electoral process, they accused him of lying.

Christie, who objected fruitlessly to what he considered hear-say evidence about the students' remarks, asked Hoeksema in cross-examination if the students were upset about Keegstra's dismissal. Were they venting their anger at you? he asked. Hoeksema said the students considered the firing unjust, but weren't rebellious.

Exchanges between the two became increasingly sarcastic as Christie accused Hoeksema of having a selective memory about what the students said. MacKenzie stepped in to calm things when he felt the questions were becoming too personal. Still, Christie continued in the same vein. He suggested Hoeksema's memory had improved between the preliminary hearing and the trial. No, said the witness, the judge at the preliminary hearing had told him to limit his statements to those he could attribute to specific students. Such was not the case here.

"What you're sure of and what you're not sure of you can't tell us for sure, can you?" Christie asked.

"I'm not sure I understand what your question is," Hoeksema retorted.

Referring often to his large, blue, ring binder, Christie tried to paint Hoeksema into a corner. Hadn't he espoused his own Christianity in the classroom and told students he expected them to be Christians too? Just like Keegstra?

Fraser argued the religious questions were irrelevant. But Christie, in the chiding tone a parent might use with a particularly dim child, said the questions were meant to show Hoeksema behaved no differently from Keegstra. Both had expressed their opinions and urged students to adopt them.

Hoeksema bridled at suggestions he had been trying to gather dirt on Keegstra to ensure he would keep his predecessor's job.

"You may not suggest that because it's not true," Hoeksema said, adding he had offers of jobs elsewhere and, in fact, left the school at the end of the term.

Then began the parade of students. It would take more than five weeks for the entire procession to pass. The tedious, often repetitive testimony and the predictable lines of cross-examination with each of the 23 witnesses was a gruelling exercise, but one Fraser later said could not be avoided.

"It had to be done because we didn't know what was coming in the defence."

In reality, the process didn't overshoot the Crown's four-week target by much. Most of the delay was due to MacKenzie's decision to shorten daily sittings by an hour, to three and a half hours, giving the jury most of the afternoon off. Looking back, Fraser considered it a good idea, because the ponderous progression of evidence would probably have sapped the jury's stamina in full-day sittings.

Almost all the former students had notes, from one to four scribblers each. Many also had copies of tests and essays and, as the material was entered, each juror was given a personal set of copies. Fraser considered the judge's decision to give the material to the jury—which was allowed without protest by the defence—a small but definite advantage to the Crown.

The first student to testify, Stephen Lecerf, had no notes. Lecerf was in the final social studies class taught by Keegstra and completed it under Hoeksema. Lercerf said Keegstra didn't follow the assigned text, but instead brought in his own material. There was little in the course which did not deal with the efforts of a Zionist-Jewish conspiracy to gain world power, Lecerf testified. The roots of the plot lay with Adam Weishaupt, an obscure Bavarian thinker who had made a pact with the Devil and who revealed his plan for world domination on May 1, 1776, a date, Lecerf said, which was still celebrated in socialist countries. The conspiracy worked through the French Revolution, communism and socialism, and is active to the present day, he said.

"Trudeau's one of their pawns," Lecerf, a nervous and slightly furtive, slim young man, told the prosecutor. "They manipulate the U.S. government, they're in control of the Russian government; I believe they're in control of France and England and, I guess, China too."

Lecerf, who at the time of his testimony was making up high school courses at Red Deer College, was less than articulate, but he seemed to have absorbed the basic theme of Keegstra's teaching: Jewish conspirators operated behind the scenes through dupes and lackeys who were not necessarily Jewish themselves.

Not all Jews were involved in the conspiracy and Keegstra had the students distinguish between two types of Jews—the Zionist Jew and something Lecerf called the Christian Jew. The Jewish religion itself was evil. The conspirators sought to manipulate the Christian way of life through financial pressure, politics, the media and the judicial system. The plotters encouraged divorce, abortion and immorality in a bid to undermine social values. Lecerf said the Talmud was the source of the conspiracy's beliefs. He had never actually seen a copy of the Talmud, however.

Lecerf said that after Keegstra was fired, the students discussed his unsuccessful appeal to the Board of Reference with Hoeksema. They suggested Jewish manipulation was responsible for their former teacher's downfall.

"That's how much control the Zionists already had of the situation," said Lecerf. "We were pointing that out to Mr. Hoeksema."

Christie used Lecerf's cross-examination both to discredit the image Hoeksema had painted of Keegstra's handiwork and to

*Zionist leader and later President of Israel, Chaim Weizmann. Keegstra believed and taught his students that Weizmann had access to many world leaders because he was a prime mover in the Zionist conspiracy. (Camera Press London photo)*

set before the jury another picture, that of a teacher leading students in search of the truth.

Keegstra was always straightforward and honest with students, Lecerf told the defence lawyer. He took a sincere interest in their concerns, even outside the classroom.

"He was like a friend you could talk to about just about anything," the witness recalled.

Hoeksema, on the other hand, seemed to the students to be less than honest. Lecerf said the teacher kept harping on Keegstra's ideas to the point where some students suspected him of being a school board spy. MacKenzie derailed the line of questioning, ruling that hearsay evidence about Hoeksema's intentions was not admissible. Still, Christie had managed to leave the impression that while his client was a font of wisdom, Hoeksema was just another functionary sent to ride herd on the inquiring young minds Keegstra had nurtured.

As he would with all the plainly pro-Keegstra students, Christie served up his questions slow and fat. However, sometimes Lecerf swung and missed.

Didn't Mr. Keegstra say nobody had a monopoly on the truth? Christie asked.

"What's a monopoly," Lecerf wanted to know.

Do you bear any animosity towards the Jews? Christie tried later.

"Animosity? Is that hatred? No," came the reply.

After Lecerf—with a few important exceptions—the student testimony fell into a numbing routine. Fraser would ask them to sketch life in Keegstra's classroom to the best of their recollections. Then he would introduce their writings, with the witnesses reading salient passages. In cross-examination, Christie would assail the accuracy of the notes and their memories. He tried to diminish the image of Keegstra as an obsessive anti-Semite, as implied by the notes. With sympathetic students he stressed Keegstra's Christian principles.

Cain Ramstead proved to be Keegstra's most articulate apologist. Tall, stocky and self-assured, Ramstead drew the fine distinctions he perceived in Keegstra's theory of the conspiracy. The most important was that the Jews of today were not Jews at all, but descendants of a Turkish ethnic group called Khazars, whose empire flourished in medieval Russia, but vanished by the 10th century AD. The Khazars had converted to Judaism and their descendants comprise most modern-day Jews, Ramstead said. Throughout his testimony, Ramstead referred to the conspirators as those "who had adopted the Jewish religion." The distinction was critical to the defence, for Keegstra had taught that modern Jews have no link to the biblical heritage of the ancient Hebrews and thus no claim to a homeland in Palestine.

Ramstead said Keegstra referred to the Khazars as self-styled Jews and imposters who adopted the tenets of the Talmud. These doctrines, Keegstra said, anointed Jews as a superior race which could murder, rob and cheat non-Jews, especially Christians, with impunity.

Although Keegstra offered evidence to back his claims, he never forced his beliefs on students, Ramstead said.

"It was put to us. We could take it or leave it."

Ramstead contradicted classmate Marla Scott, who preceded him on the stand and who said the conspiracy theory surfaced almost daily in class. Ramstead said Keegstra discussed the origins of modern-day Jews in few classes and only touched on the conspiracy theory in relation to historical events. He said Keegstra distinguished between so-called Big Jews—the international capitalists "making heaps and heaps of money and having heaps and heaps of wealth and power"—and Little Jews, who where unaware of the conspiracy and would have disapproved of it. The conspiracy involved only a small percentage of Jews at the very top, Ramstead explained.

Ramstead's notes were the first to be entered by the Crown. Christie made a futile attempt to have the notebooks thrown out as evidence. He argued they were not an accurate record of what Keegstra had said and, as such, could not be used as evidence against him.

Had that motion succeeded, Christie would have torpedoed the Crown's case then and there. But MacKenzie ruled the notes were Ramstead's interpretation of what he was taught. The weight of this evidence in determining the verdict would be up to the jury to decide.

Ramstead outlined how the first class dealt with what Keegstra called the problem of truth; the need to interpret facts and try to arrange them in coherent, logical patterns to arrive at the truth. Facts by themselves are cold and meaningless. Inferences must be drawn from them and subjected to the total witness of one's experience. If the facts are applied to a theory and do not fit, then the theory has to be revised. This philosophical grounding showed up in almost all the student's notes.

The notes were a survey of Western history from England in the 1600s—when Keegstra taught that Jews began to take over the economy—through the formation of Jewish-controlled secret societies such as the Illuminati and the Freemasons, to communism, the spearhead of revolution which was to lead to one world government and a new world order.

When a reference needed clarification, Ramstead readily obliged. Hands clasped behind him or resting casually in front, his voice clear and firm, he said the conspirators were using secular humanism to erode Christian society. The Illuminati used the "Golden Anvil" of international finance and the hammer of revolution in an effort to crush the Western middle class.

Zionism was the conspiracy's most modern manifestation, aimed at acquiring Palestine as a homeland for the Jews. Zionists had created anti-Semitism as a means of gaining sympathy to further their aims, he said.

Fraser and Phillippe knew from the start they could expect many of the students to disown what they had written years before. Still, they hoped that the notes and essays would speak for themselves.

Ramstead was a gold nugget for the defence. Christie opened his cross-examination by asking what Ramstead was doing now. The young witness replied he was studying journalism in Calgary. He had planned to become a teacher but thought better of it.

"If a teacher said something that was not popular, he would be fired and crucified, as it were."

Most pro-Keegstra students were simply expected to agree with Christie as he posed long, detailed questions, but Ramstead went beyond that, offering his own elaborations.

He said he felt his notes were only about 40-percent accurate. He could have written a lot more detail about what Keegstra meant when he referred to Jews in class. He was pointing to Bolshevik, Zionist and Khazar Jews, the conspirators, not ordinary Jews. It was ridiculous to suggest Keegstra preached hatred.

"He always said that to hate is not to be Christian," said Ramstead.

Keegstra made it clear he was teaching an alternative view of history, an unofficial, unpopular theory which could ultimately cost him his job, Ramstead said. By the time Ramstead took Keegstra's course, the teacher had been warned by the school board to stop teaching the conspiracy as fact.

Muzzling Keegstra was a victory for the conspirators and would hasten the advent of world government, Ramstead said.

"That's about what people believe will happen if the ideas of Mr. Keegstra are destroyed."

Ramstead also drew a distinction which the defence felt would absolve Keegstra from the charge of promoting hatred against a group. Keegstra was condemning the actions of the conspirators, Ramstead explained, not the Jewish people as a whole.

When students were less compliant, Christie tried to force them to recant their direct testimony or at least qualify it. Some, like Paul Maddox, had faced the waspish defence lawyer before and seemed to prefer to end the ordeal as soon as possible.

Maddox, who practised martial arts tai chi movements in the courthouse hallway to relax between appearances, told Fraser that Keegstra had announced at the start of the Grade 9 social studies class: "This year I'm going to try to get you to believe in the right things."

Christie, in his cross-examination, began to pick at inconsistencies between Maddox's testimony at the preliminary hearing and his statements at the trial. Maddox put the differences down to his nervousness when questioned by Christie at the 1984 hearing.

"When do you tell the truth?" asked Christie. "When you're nervous for the Crown or nervous for the defence?"

"I just wanted to get it over with," the teenager admitted.

Christie accused him of twisting Keegstra's words. Maddox, off balance, said he wasn't sure how some of his notes were related. When Keegstra said he wanted to get students thinking right, wasn't he referring to the need to analyse facts to find the truth? Christie asked.

"Yes, it's possible," said Maddox.

The frail-looking 16-year-old took a chair as Christie pressed on. Soon he was agreeing to a litany of Keegstra's attributes as a teacher. Maddox said he enjoyed the class, got on well with his teacher and derived more from the course than from any other he took that year. He also acknowledged he felt under pressure from the Crown, the media and his mother, who Christie suggested had hated Keegstra for a long time.

While his former student testified, Keegstra sat quietly, rarely looking at the witness. He took notes, stared at the empty walls and idly chewed on a pen.

Fraser salvaged something from Maddox in re-examination. Maddox said the pressure he confessed to feeling was to remember what he had been taught and to remember how his notes related to what Keegstra had said.

"That's the pressure I mean."

Three young women broke down on the stand under Christie's relentless demands for precision and accuracy in their recollections. Trudi Roth, pregnant at the time, stood by her testimony that if a passage was in her notes, Keegstra must have said it.

"I was so busy then, trying to get down what Mr. Keegstra was saying, I didn't have time to get down my own interpretations."

She withstood Christie's attacks on her truthfulness and intelligence.

"If I'm not absolutely sure that Mr. Keegstra said that at one time or another, I would not tell you that he did," she insisted at one point.

"Do you understand how important it is to be accurate?" Christie asked, but Roth, already crying, could only sob.

After a 30-minute recess while she regained her composure,

Roth returned, red-eyed, and testified to Keegstra's overall sincerity and commitment to truth.

But Christie could not penetrate the wall of bitterness which surrounded Roth's classmate Lorriene Bogdane. Bogdane, hurt by what she felt was Keegstra's personal dislike for her, would not concede the attributes other students had ascribed to the teacher. She was ignored in class, she said. Keegstra never asked her any questions and she never volunteered any answers. She started skipping class towards the end of the year and ultimately failed the course. The teaching, she said, was very definitely aimed at the Jews.

"He didn't like them very much and he more or less taught us we shouldn't like them either."

She had been given a 45-percent grade for an essay on Zionism, which she said she had plagiarized from an encyclopedia. Keegstra had dotted the paper with comments such as "built up by the Jewish press," and "your information comes from the propagandistic World Book." She said a true-false test contained a question asking whether Jews generally were good citizens. The correct answer was false.

She said Keegstra believed what he was saying: "He would, like, preach Billy Graham-style."

Christie chose to confront this unsympathetic witness head on. After court broke for the day, he had Bogdane followed. It was not the last time he would report on the out-of-court activities of a participant in the trial. The next day he asked Bogdane if, over lunch, she had told her friend Trudi Roth that while she had testified her notes were verbatim from Keegstra's dictation, she had in fact added her own material.

Bogdane denied Christie's account of her remarks and MacKenzie shut off the line of questioning. But the incident had left the scent of perjury in the nostrils of the jury.

From then on, it was open war between the lawyer and the witness. Bogdane smirked at some of Christie's questions and sneered at him as he delved through his notes.

"You didn't particularly like Mr. Keegstra, did you?" Christie asked.

"Only because he had a particular dislike for me," Bogdane replied.

Her anger increasingly evident, Bogdane's flippant answers only underscored Christie's point. This witness, he would say later, obviously hated Keegstra enough to skew her testimony in the Crown's favor. In reality, her understanding of the class material was limited, and the meanings she took from some of her notes were pure imagination, he concluded.

Fraser stepped in to protect his witness, saying cross-examination had gone beyond the bounds of reason. But MacKenzie said it was legitimate for Christie to probe the connection between the Jewish references in the notes and Bogdane's understanding of Keegstra's teaching.

Despite the battering, Bogdane in the end did not back away from her feeling that Keegstra did not like Jews.

"He was trying to get it across to us that they were bad. That's what I got out of his class at the end of that year."

While students such as Bogdane and Ramstead were known quantities, no one was prepared for Kelly Cordon, whose testimony zinged the defence.

The tall, thin, soft-spoken 22-year-old, who had no obvious axe to grind, was a sleeper.

Cordon told assistant prosecutor Larry Phillippe that Keegstra only referred in passing to theories that didn't mesh with his own ideas.

"He might tell you what the generally accepted theory of history is and then he'd tell us what really happened," said Cordon.

The Jews, Keegstra taught, were responsible for fostering the master race theory and pan-Germanism in 19th-century Germany as a means of entrenching themselves with the ruling elite, especially Bismarck, the German chancellor. During periodic upheavals in Europe, Jewish-led thugs and revolutionaries —so-called gutter rats—pillaged and tortured. (All the students' notes showed Keegstra seemed fascinated with atrocities and perversion, describing massacres, mutilations and the orgiastic behavior of the evil conspirators in fine detail.) Most importantly, Keegstra traced the origins of the conspiracy back to the Pharisees of the Bible.

"It was their religion that they were eventually to take over the world," said Cordon.

More bombshells fell in cross-examination. Christie launched his familiar attack on Cordon's recollections and his understanding of the classes, but the witness, who paused thoughtfully between answers, would not budge.

"Did he encourage you to think for yourself?" Christie asked.

"I'd have to say no to that," came the reply. Other theories would be studied, but "when it came time to write a test or essay, it had to be supporting the conspiracy theory."

A student could discuss things in class, but would always be put down by Keegstra if the comments deviated from the teacher's views. Cordon said he kept quiet in class.

Christie tried to work Cordon back onside with other students but succeeded only in digging himself and his client in deeper. The conspiracy didn't originate with Jews, did it? he asked. No, said Cordon, but Keegstra was discussing the question of evil and evil always came from the Jews. In Cordon's notes, the name of nearly every person labelled evil carried the notation "Jew" beside it in brackets. The course pointed to a conspiracy of Zionist Jews out to rule the world, said Cordon.

Christie tried another angle.

Wasn't Keegstra speaking only of a certain elite group? Yes, said Cordon, but "as I recall, the greatest majority were Jews."

Christie tried again.

Didn't Keegstra espouse Christian principles? Yes, said Cordon.

"Then again, he would turn around and there would be all this hatred in our notes."

It was clear that Cordon had made up his mind about Keegstra's teachings, but Christie, instead of getting him off the stand and away from the jury, persisted in trying to find a loophole, something to repair the damage being done. Wasn't Keegstra really criticizing wicked deeds?

"It didn't always come out that clearly in his class," said Cordon. "I'm telling you that it implied hate to me."

"Without the deed, where's the hate?" asked Christie.

Then why list peoples' race and religion beside their names? Cordon shot back. Why continuously make it clear that it was Jews who were doing all these bad things?

Cordon insisted that his notes, in point form, provided a clear understanding for him of what went on in the classroom. Christie, unable to shake Cordon on the notes, made a personal attack. The lawyer suggested Cordon felt a certain animosity towards Keegstra because of a sewer right-of-way dispute the student's father had with Keegstra while the former teacher was mayor of Eckville.

"I don't see what my father has got to do with my social studies class," Cordon replied.

"I'm not suggesting you're trying to deceive anybody," Christie said wearily. "I'm suggesting your notes don't record what was said at the time."

Cordon maintained they were accurate and that he saw hate on every page of the notes.

Phillippe, in re-examination, seized the unlooked-for opportunity. The prosecution had been taken by surprise, since Cordon had given no indication of his feelings in three pretrial interviews.

Phillippe asked for examples of hatred and Cordon obliged.

He leafed through his notes to passages that said Jews owned the banks and the factories, Jews were cruel, Jews never worked and Jews lived well off the labor of others.

Cordon also recalled the true-false question about the good citizenship of Jews.

"You couldn't help presuming it was all Jews."

The jury was to hear 15 more students after Cordon, but his combination of sincerity and calm had an impact far beyond that of the others.

Their testimony was mixed. They read notes which blandly discussed the manifold crimes of Jewish-led conspirators and essays advocating getting rid of Jews. They also displayed genuine admiration and respect for Keegstra as a teacher.

Gwen Matthews, who had been confined to a wheelchair after a 1980 accident involving a drunk driver, accepted Keegstra at face value.

"There never was hatred promoted against anyone," she said. "As a matter of fact, he promoted positive values."

She said references to Jews in her notes were a handy short-hand for specific types such as Bolsheviks and Zionists.

An essay about the dangers of Judaism was not meant as an indictment of Jews in general: "The wicked, evil conspirators, who either had Jewish roots in them, Communists, Bolsheviks, Zionists or plain sadism, succeeded through the years to ruin or almost ruin many countries through smearing Christians, spreading lies and betraying people. They have corrupted minds, damaged morals and caused much hatred. Today, it is still practised." The essay earned Matthews a mark of 85 percent.

Christie used Matthews, who was on the stand three days, to enter a few exhibits of his own, including an essay she had written on the ideal society. The paper—with another 85-percent grade—in a nutshell described a utopia where people would be prosperous and God-fearing in an economy built around Social Credit and where there would be no liquor stores. Drunk drivers would be severely punished.

"I hope some day Christianity will reign over the globe," she concluded.

"It will," Keegstra wrote on the paper. "But it will be a new heaven on earth."

Fraser, in re-examination, did not let the reference go unremarked. Did her ideal society leave any place for Jews? he asked.

"Not in that context," Matthews replied.

In spite of her innocent utopianism, Matthews' credibility

took some punishment. She told Christie she felt pressured to tell RCMP investigators in 1983 that everything Keegstra said related to Jews.

"There is no international Jewish conspiracy," and Keegstra never said there was, she told Christie.

Fraser, though, produced her original, signed police statement. It said Keegstra taught about the conspiracy in both Grade 9 and 12, and that she believed there was a conspiracy "that some Jews are involved in." She admitted to the Crown that when she made the statement to police she did not feel pressured and could have elaborated on her answer at the time, if she had chosen to.

Throughout the testimony of the students, Fraser sought to play down as irrelevant Keegstra's apparent distinctions between Jewish conspirators and Jews in general. Danny Desrosiers said conspiratorial groups such as the Bolsheviks took on the Jewish religion as a rationale for their actions, using its beliefs to justify their power plays.

"What do you call people of the Judaic faith?" Fraser asked.

"Jews," said Desrosiers.

Such answers gave Fraser the confidence to risk canceling a plan to call an expert on anti-Semitism who was to add context to some of the derogatory references to Jews and put the conspiracy theory into perspective. However, he decided that the notes, tests and essays had established the connection to anti-Semitism so clearly that he could dispense with the expert, a University of Toronto professor.

Instead, he asked MacKenzie to take judicial notice of the fact that Judaism is the religion of the Jews and that, conversely, Jews were a group identified by the practice of Judaism. Such an offical ruling would underscore the pejorative references to Jews—no matter how they were hyphenated—and Judaism in the students' material. The defence would find it more difficult to argue Keegstra was pointing to only a small percentage of Jews or was criticizing the works of imposters who adopted the Jewish religion.

Christie was caught off guard by Fraser's request. He had planned to challenge the expert's credentials.

The next day, the Friday of the sixth week of the trial, MacKenzie listened to arguments in the absence of the jury. Fraser contended the link between Judaism and people known as Jews is common knowledge, spelled out clearly in standard reference books such as encyclopedias. Under the rules of governing this type of judicial ruling, MacKenzie need look no further in assessing the validity of the statements, said Fraser.

Christie argued the connection was far from clear and produced a stack of books and articles which he said showed the
definition of who is a Jew and what constitutes Judaism are far
from clear and have always been in dispute. Interestingly,
Christie relied in part on encyclopedias which his client claimed
were censored by the conspiracy. MacKenzie, who had taken
longer to rule on minor points of the law, quickly settled the
matter in the Crown's favor.

"I am satisfied there is a religion called Judaism," the judge
said. "I am also satisfied Judaism is the religion of the group we
commonly know as the Jewish people." Jews may have other
distinguishing characteristics, but their religion "is the one sure
way of identifying the Jewish people."

But Fraser lost a round, too, when MacKenzie agreed to bar
testimony from a social psychologist on grounds it might
unduly prejudice the jury's ability to assess the evidence on its
own. The Crown had planned to call Dr. Brendan Rule of the
University of Alberta to give evidence on the likely impact of
Keegstra's teaching on his students. Christie argued the indictment specified promotion of hatred, not the acquisition of
hatred by the students. Fraser, who himself had said the
acquisition was not germane to proving the charge, countered
that Rule's testimony would help the jury determine whether
Keegstra's teaching could have caused hatred. As well, it would
give them an insight into how teaching techniques had been
employed in the class.

MacKenzie ruled that experts are called when a jury of ordinary people need help in assessing matters normally beyond
their knowledge. Hatred was something any person could
determine.

In fact, the question of what constitutes hatred was one on
which the defence would expend much argument later in the
proceedings.

The judge's ruling seemed not to be based on arguments
raised by Christie, and Fraser said later he would have pressed
more forcefully for Rule's acceptance had he known MacKenzie
would decide on his own hook, rather than on the defence
presentation.

"It was evidence that would have assisted the jury," Fraser
said. "There was a hole [in the Crown's case] and I had to close
that hole in summation."

The Crown's final witness was Robert David, school superintendent for the Lacombe County Board of Education, the man
who had investigated the Ackerman and Maddox complaints
against Keegstra. Christie succeeded in limiting David's testi-

mony on the ground that much of what went on between David and Keegstra would be hearsay and that since Keegstra was a subordinate of David's while teaching, Keegstra might have felt compelled to answer the superintendent's questions. In effect, it would mean Keegstra was being forced to testify against himself through David.

The ruling watered down much of what David had to say. The only substantive material involved two sentences in letters sent to Keegstra. They followed up on a verbal directive to Keegstra to stop teaching the conspiracy as fact. Five other letters were ruled inadmissible.

"The Jewish conspiracy theory must not be taught as if it were fact instead of just another view of history," said a letter dated December 18, 1981, the day David met Keegstra in Eckville.

Later, after the school board met in February, another letter warned: "You must not teach discriminatory theories as if they were fact. This is particularly applicable to the Jewish conspiracy theory of history."

Christie managed to provoke more than one rise out of the volatile David, whose voice rose in anger when Christie suggested he had tried to intimidate Keegstra's defenders in the school and sent photocopies of the offending notebooks to Jewish groups as part of a smear campaign against the teacher. Both allegations were strongly denied by David, as was a suggestion Hoeksema had been hired to ferret out more dirt against Keegstra from the students.

On May 22, the 31st day of the trial, the Crown rested its case, satisfied that the notes, essays, tests and testimony had made an impact on the jury.

As the methodical production of evidence had progressed, spectator interest dwindled. The once-full courtroom now held only 20 or so regulars, most of them Keegstra's diehard supporters. In addition, a half-dozen reporters stuck it through, searching for fresh angles to the repetitive notes. Jurors, spectators and reporters sometimes nodded off in the stuffy courtroom as spring wore slowly toward summer.

One man who did not snooze was Jim Keegstra. His face remained impassive as his students testified, although sometimes a smile escaped when a former pupil said something amusing or endearing. The young witnesses sometimes tried to catch his eye, but he didn't return their glances.

"How could I look at a student, especially those kids that were for me?" he pondered. "I had to be careful I didn't look at them or Fraser would accuse me of coaching. Those that were against me, how could I look at them? I had to sit tight, passively. I couldn't show my emotions.

"I felt sorry for them, quite honestly. They were drug up there. It is an evil and perverse situation that they were drug up there against their will."

Not surprisingly, after Fraser rested his case, Christie entered a motion of no evidence, arguing for dismissal of the case because none of the witnesses had testified to the promotion of hatred. The motion failed.

The following day, Christie, looking tired and drawn, stepped out to begin Keegstra's defence.

"I will be presenting evidence to show no hatred was promoted," he told the jury, "and that some element of success is necessary to justify a conviction."

The Crown, he said, had alleged thousands of instances and events that wilfully promoted hatred. He felt obligated to rebut them.

"I hope you'll be patient with me. I have to answer everything the Crown has put before you in some way or another."

Christie outlined his arguments, which he had sketched during his cross-examinations of the Crown witnesses. Keegstra was not wilfully promoting hatred, but teaching the truth as he saw it. He encouraged inquiry among his students and promoted understanding and thought.

What is hate? Christie asked. It was not hateful to demonstrate something about the Talmud. Its concepts and ideas could be criticized without condemning the whole Jewish religion. Keegstra's teachings had not been directed against all Jews, but against specific concepts, actions and ideas.

The notes should not be accepted as accurate representations of Keegstra's classes, he said. Students had taken their own meanings from what Keegstra had said and some were completely unreasonable. Keegstra had taught more than 200 students over the years; the jury had heard notes from about 20, all carefully selected by the Crown.

He outlined the defences. The law allowed Keegstra to make hateful statements if they were true, if they were opinions given in good faith on a religious subject, if they were matters of public interest discussed for the public good and he had reasonable grounds to believe they were true, or if they were intended to remove hatred. All applied to Keegstra, Christie said.

"Sincerity and honesty are pretty major factors in assessing what Mr. Keegstra was talking about," said the defence lawyer.

Christie said his client had lost his job and been ejected from his profession. He had lost his bid for a second term as mayor of Eckville. Now the Crown, in trying to make him a criminal, also wanted to stifle him. Free speech was at stake.

You are grappling with a historic issue, Christie told the jurors. The verdict "will determine the history and future of a great many people."

Christie began by calling six character witnesses, five of them Keegstra's former teaching colleagues from Eckville. Unfailingly, they testified to Keegstra's generosity, teaching talent and overall high standing as a man of Christian principles in both the school and the community. But none could swear to any real knowledge of what went on in Keegstra's social studies classes. Their contribution to the defence was of doubtful value. But as became clear at the end of the trial, they may have helped keep Keegstra out of jail.

Mild-mannered Joseph Lindberg, a teacher for 32 years who taught social studies to Grade 11 students at Eckville, said he and Keegstra were at opposite ends of the political spectrum. However, he praised Keegstra for impeccable honesty and renowned generosity.

"His home is a refuge for outcasts from prisons. He befriended and championed the cause of widows," Lindberg said to snickers from the gallery.

Keegstra, he said, always had time for others, whether it was helping people lay sidewalks or just listening to their cares. He was "a supporter in times of travail and distress."

Was there any racial hatred evident in Keegstra? Christie asked. On the contrary, Lindberg said. He welcomed other races into his home.

"I've seen the igloo in front of his house that was put there by a master craftsman from the Arctic," Lindberg said.

Among the prison "outcasts" who enjoyed Keegstra's hospitality were men Lindberg called "Gerry the Indian" and "Albert the Eskimo." Lindberg said he never saw "Bob the Jew" in Keegstra's house, but he had seen him in the family's car.

Fraser interrupted to question the relevance of Lindberg's opinions of Keegstra's character, but MacKenzie agreed with Christie that if wilfulness was an issue, character was an integral part of the defence.

Lindberg said he and Keegstra often argued politics in the staff room, but remained personal friends.

"He kept me entertained," said Lindberg. "But I'm not aware that he changed me."

Lindberg, who had been the school's principal between 1970 and 1975, said he accepted Keegstra as a "straight-laced, puritanical Christian."

He said Keegstra's firing hit the school hard.

"There was almost a mood of hysteria in the building. Everyone was in a state of distress. We thought they were out to get us. We thought we were under attack."

A majority of the students signed a petition calling for Keegstra's reinstatement. Others vented their spleens on his successor, Dick Hoeksema. At one point, students came to class wearing swastikas, but it was only in fun, Lindberg said.

"That's a pretty weird sort of fun, isn't it?" Fraser asked in cross-examination.

Lindberg said the students were dedicated to Keegstra, but he saw no evidence Keegstra had produced in them a partiality for the Nazis. He said he occasionally saw things which Keegstra wrote on the blackboard, but never saw any students' notes or essays and recalled nothing critical of the Jews. He was aware, though, that Keegstra was "inordinately critical of Russians."

Fraser's tone became more demanding as he questioned Lindberg. When you were principal, did you not seek to have Keegstra relieved of his responsibilities for social studies? Lindberg admitted he had arranged to have Keegstra transferred from social studies, but then he himself was transferred temporarily to another school. When he returned, as an ordinary teacher, not as principal, he found Keegstra still teaching social studies.

In the rapid-fire exchange that followed, it never became clear why Lindberg was troubled by Keegstra's teaching of social studies if the only complaints he had received dealt with Keegstra's treatment of the Russians.

"I was afraid of the community reaction," Lindberg said. "I wanted him transferred out of the course so I wouldn't have to answer to what he was teaching."

Lindberg told of conversations with Keegstra and of books students showed him, such as *None Dare Call It Treason* and *None Dare Call It Conspiracy*, tracts which claimed a Hidden Hand controlled world affairs. Lindberg described them as "foolish little books."

Lindberg admitted to Fraser that he hadn't wanted his own children to take social studies from Keegstra. Christie would not leave the reference to Lindberg's children hanging and the witness conceded that one of his two daughters did take the class, apparently without effect.

"Quite the reverse," he said. "For reasons I do not know, she seemed to acquire an affection for Jews."

Mathematics and science teacher Kenneth Bradshaw said he had known Keegstra more than eight years.

"I respected the man a great deal. I still do. He's a very honest person, perhaps the most honest person I know."

But Bradshaw admitted to Fraser that he had attended two meetings of the Canadian League of Rights, whose affiliate, the Canadian Intelligence Service, was the source of much of the anti-Semitic material Keegstra used. One of the meetings was held in the school itself, where students assembled in the auditorium to hear Patrick Walsh, the League's research director, discuss the new Canadian Constitution.

Bradshaw recalled one reference to Jews at the second meeting in Red Deer, which took place after Keegstra had been fired. One man said the "smear" against Keegstra was to be expected, because he criticized the Jews. Bradshaw said he glanced over a display of pamphlets for sale but had no real interest in them. He said he saw none of Keegstra's students at the Red Deer meeting.

Clarence Koots, a former Keegstra student and onetime Eckville teacher who had joined the RCMP, also testified to Keegstra's good character. Standing in the witness box, hands clasped at the small of his back, Koots looked like a policeman giving evidence as he said Keegstra promoted a lot of thought in his class and provoked discussion among the students. He said Keegstra broached the Zionist-Jewish conspiracy when Koots was in Grade 12 in 1974. The teacher said the plot took in only a small portion of the Jewish community. Koots, under cross-examination, could not recall details of the class but said what did stand out in his memory was the emphasis on the conspiracy.

Some of the most curious testimony came from Edwin Olsen, Lindberg's successor as principal. Like the others, he attested to Keegstra's high standing in the town and the school. He planned his lessons well, enforced discipline in his classes and was well liked by his students.

What was Keegstra's general attitude toward tolerance? Christie asked.

"I never heard him call any group down as such, except maybe Communists, or maybe Zionists," said Olsen.

The two teachers shared a congenial personal relationship and Olsen was satisfied with Keegstra's teaching methods after monitoring two of his courses—a drafting class and a Grade 9 social studies class in the fall of 1982. At the time, Keegstra seemed to be using the authorized text, said Olsen.

The principal testified there was room in the social studies curriculum topic areas to allow discussion of matters related to Jews. The curriculum guide outlined general headings such as co-operation and conflict and told teachers to address such topics as the Russian Revolution, the world wars and the formation of Israel. But it gave no specific directions on how these were to be taught. Teachers could express their opinions and debate was encouraged.

Olsen said he had no evidence hatred was promoted in Keegstra's classroom. His own children—including daughter Rhonda who testified at the trial—went through Keegstra's courses, and he had no complaints about what they were taught.

In cross-examination, it became obvious Olsen had no overt misgivings about Keegstra, even after he came under the scrutiny of the school superintendent. Part of the problem, Olsen explained, was the workload. As principal, he still taught a full course load, and Education Department policy left the job of teacher evaluation and the handling of parental complaints to the district superintendent.

Olsen said he became aware of some of the essays from Keegstra's classes, but could not recall being alarmed by them. There had been no files on Keegstra or any other teacher when Olsen took over from Lindberg, and even when a couple of complaints about Keegstra's teachings on Roman Catholics surfaced in 1976 and 1978, Olsen kept no record of them. They had been handled by the previous superintendent, Frank Flanagan, and "at the time it didn't seem like a serious issue."

By 1981, Olsen had become aware of some material and references to matters which might be misconstrued. He read the essay by Danny Desrosiers which Keegstra had shown to Robert David. The paper warned that Jews were dangerous and must be put in their place.

"At the time, I was wondering why he wrote what he wrote," said the quiet-spoken principal. Even after the 1981 incident, though, Olsen saw no need to monitor Keegstra more closely.

"At this point it was already like in the hands of the superintendent."

Olsen was concerned but, as with the 1976 and 1978 incidents, this matter did not appear that serious.

Desrosiers' essay dealt with Jews and history, a legitimate topic, Olsen said.

"To me, it expresses a viewpoint that a certain group is out to get the other group at all costs," said Olsen.

Christie's final character witness was William Zuidhof, a Lacombe-area farmer who, as a member of the county board of education, voted to retain Keegstra. Christie admitted later that Zuidhof was a "filler" witness, who had been sitting innocently in the public gallery watching the trial earlier in the day. A court official, aware he was to testify, had hustled him out, as witnesses are normally excluded from the proceedings until they have given their evidence. Zuidhof said he was unaware until the previous evening that he would be called and did not know of the exclusion rule, which Christie had forgotten to mention to him.

Zuidhof had little to offer beyond the now-standard testament to Keegstra's character and his "vast knowledge" of world events. But he was available for cross-examination.

"Do you hold the same views as Mr. Keegstra about Jews," asked Fraser after Christie was finished.

"Not necessarily," Zuidhof replied. When pressed, though, he admitted to "more or less" the same views. He qualified that by adding he was concerned about a political conspiracy of Zionists, not one involving the average Jew.

Christie had to fight to get his final witness on the stand. Fraser objected to the calling of Heather Botting, wife of Keegstra ally Gary Botting. She was a socio-cultural anthropologist. Christie wanted her to testify about the theory that modern Jews are not related to the Jews of the Bible but are descended from the Turko-Finnish Khazars.

Fraser said MacKenzie's ruling regarding Jews and Judaism should bar testimony on the origins of Jews, but Christie said that should have no bearing on Keegstra's understanding of the theory or on his right to defend himself on the basis of truth or reasonable ground for belief.

"My client has every right to demonstrate that he had a reasonable basis for his belief that the Jewish people are not an identifiable group pertaining to religion," said Christie.

The two sides spent an afternoon battling over Botting's credentials.

Botting, small and slim, with thigh-length raven hair, specialized in the anthropology of religion. It was learned she also dabbled in the occult as part of what her husband called her inside research on religions.

The Bottings were co-authors of a book on their former religion entitled *The Orwellian World of the Jehovah's Witnesses.*

Heather Botting, in the absence of the jury, told the court she became familiar with the theory of the Khazars during her research into the concept of the Chosen People, an idea also adopted by the Jehovah's Witnesses. She said the Khazars migrated to Western Europe from southern Russia after the breakup of their medieval empire. Her research was buttressed by philosopher Arthur Koestler's book *The Thirteenth Tribe.*

Fraser denigrated her command of the subject in cross-examination. He had her admit she had read only one book and a few articles relating to Khazars. She also acknowledged Koestler had been writing outside his field.

The theory was not supported by other scholars, Fraser said. That may be so, Botting conceded, but it was not insupportable and therefore merited investigation.

MacKenzie waited until the following week before deciding that Botting could testify. Although he ruled she was not an expert, he would allow her to give evidence, not to prove the theory, but to show how Keegstra acquired his beliefs. That decision set the stage for the introduction of a welter of books, pamphlets and articles on the same basis. Keegstra would later offer them as evidence of the reasonableness of his belief in the conspiracy theory. All were admitted on grounds they helped form and support his ideas, not that they were true.

Botting spent little more time on the stand than was involved in the legal wrangle to get her there. She told Christie the Khazars were a Turko-Finnish ethnic group which lived in the Caucasus region of Russia between AD 300 and 995. In AD 730, their king and his nobles converted to Judaism. Their empire thrived on trade between the Moslem East and the Christian West until it was overthrown by neighboring Russian tribes. A couple of works on the Khazars had been published, said Botting, but new research was being done with the translation of old records in Hebrew and Chinese.

She said some researchers believe the Khazars migrated westward after the empire fell and formed the nucleus of the modern Ashkenazi, or eastern European Jews. Conventional theory holds that the Ashkenazi developed from Jews chased east from central and western Europe by anti-Semitism.

With the jury back, Fraser developed his attack on Botting's credibility. She admitted she had done no personal research on the origins of European Jewry. Fraser suggested that was an important area of knowledge for someone speculating on the role of the Khazars. She agreed numerous groups of Jews settled in Europe following the Roman sack of Jerusalem and the destruction of the Second Temple in AD 73, but said the Khazars by the 10th century made up a large group of Jews and cannot be wished away. But, said Fraser, even Koestler acknowledged his theory was speculative, with few facts to back it.

"I would not call it pure speculation," said Botting. "I would call it a more difficult enterprise in piecing it together."

The Crown prosecutor worked at unnerving Botting. He made her pronounce Koestler's name repeatedly—she pronounced it Kersler instead of the proper Kestler—and asked her to spell it. She did, correctly. He named several books on Jewish history which she said she had not read, and she admitted she had not even read through Koestler completely.

Christie's star witness was to be Keegstra himself. But before calling his client to the stand the lawyer planned an attention-grabbing warmup—Alberta Premier Peter Lougheed. The premier, however, was fighting the subpoena.

The defence wanted Lougheed to testify about statements he had made in the legislature about intolerance in relation to the Keegstra affair and in the wake of Stephen Stiles's comments. The objective was to show how much influence the "conspiracy" had. Lougheed had received a telegram the day before his statement from Nazi-hunter Simon Wiesenthal. Lougheed, Christie said, had used his position to condemn Keegstra even before the charge was laid.

However, in a separate hearing, MacKenzie agreed with Lougheed's lawyer that the premier could add nothing relevant to the case because his comments had come 18 months after the period covered by the indictment and he had no knowledge of Keegstra or his teachings.

It was time for the principal actor to mount the stage, which he would occupy for 26 days of testimony.

It is not surprising that defence counsel and prosecutor differed on the impact of Keegstra's testimony. Christie, in his final summation, would say the jury had seen Keegstra's honesty and sincerity for themselves, seen how he came to form his ideas and seen the deep religious faith which underscored them. But given the verdict, it's more likely the jury accepted Fraser's analysis, that what they saw was a confession under oath.

Guided by Christie, Keegstra wove together the main themes of his teaching. The Jews held to an evil religion based on the Talmud, which perverted the laws of God and condoned ill treatment of non-Jews, the goyim. The Talmud justified atrocities in the name of the Chosen People, the superior race; it was the ideological core of the Hidden Hand which worked behind the scenes to institute one world government under a new world order; it fuelled the conspiracy of international financiers, mostly Jewish, and Jewish-led revolutionary movements; and it provided a rationale for the illegitimate state of Israel. The Jews were not Jews at all, but Khazars who had adopted Judaism. Therefore, anti-Semitism cannot exist because modern Jews are not even Semites. These imposters had insinuated themselves into every institution of society.

To Keegstra, nothing in the world was as it seemed. If one looked closely, one could divine the Hidden Hand at work. The answer, though, was not action, but to reveal the truth and

Calgary Herald *editorial cartoonist Vance Rodewalt illustrated the Alberta government couldn't escape the political flap surrounding the Keegstra case. Premier Peter Lougheed successfully fought a subpoena which would have forced him to testify as a defence witness. Keegstra's lawyer, Doug Christie, argued Lougheed's public statement concerning Keegstra's teaching illustrated the kind of pressure the Jewish conspiracy could bring to bear on his client. But Mr. Justice John McKenzie agreed with Lougheed's lawyer that the premier could contribute nothing to the evidence concerning what Keegstra taught before he was pulled into the limelight.* (Calgary Herald)

propagate Christian love. To be aware, and wary, of the conspiracy was apparently enough.

But there were people in Eckville who didn't want to hear the truth, who hated him for revealing it, a kind of kaffeeklatsch conspiracy of parents who had worked for years to oust him from the school. It was beyond his understanding what they had against him.

Keegstra's first days on the stand were an energetic outpouring of ideas, explanations and qualifications, nostrums, sermons and lectures. As the weeks passed, Keegstra would sometimes appear weary in the witness box, but he never seriously flagged. Nothing, though, could match the first days. It was as if a valve on a high-pressure line had been twisted open. After keeping his peace for 35 days, Keegstra was finally having his day. Indeed, except for the comparatively brief stint on the stand at the Board of Reference hearing, he had never had an opportunity to make a full, public defence. Christie, whose job it was to introduce Keegstra's defence through questions and exhibits, sometimes found himself hard-pressed to control the torrent of words from his client.

On the stand, Keegstra was engaging. His thin-lipped smile came readily as he answered questions in a folksy, unstilted manner. His eyes, never fully visible behind his photochromic, light-sensitive glasses, nevertheless became the bellwether of his feelings. They often glowed warmly when he spoke directly to the jury. The prosecutor, in cross-examination, would come to recognize the wide-eyed, zealous glare that accompanied Keegstra's more entrenched viewpoints. Sometimes watchers would catch a hint of contempt when Keegstra, looking sidelong at a questioner, dealt with the machinations of the conspiracy.

Christie would ultimately put about 150 books, articles and pamphlets into evidence, with Keegstra, like the Crown's student witnesses reading passages he considered relevant. MacKenzie allowed the exhibits on fairly narrow grounds, as indications of how Keegstra had formed his beliefs and how they supported his ideas. They would go toward the defence of reasonable grounds, the judge told the jury, but they were not to be taken as proof that what Keegstra believed was true. The goal of the defence was to convince the jury that a large body of written work existed to substantiate Keegstra's conspiracy theory and that it was therefore a legitimate topic of instruction for his social studies classes.

Aside from a rough chronological order, the introduction of the writings seemed to follow no obvious pattern. Works would be entered and Keegstra would explain his interpretations of the material, how it fit into the social studies curriculum—in his view—and why he felt the mainstream view elaborated in the text, which he rarely used in class, was unsatisfactory.

Many of the books Keegstra used in school were from his personal library, seized by the Mounties during their investigation. The books had been in the Crown's hands since mid-1983, and Christie had complained several times that they were needed to mount a proper defence. MacKenzie finally ordered Fraser and Christie to work out a system giving the defence access to the books under court supervision, but Christie and Keegstra continually reminded the jury the books had not been available for the preparation of the case.

The routine of reading from the relevant works, then elaborating on the half-dozen or so themes of the conspiracy soon became repetitious, rivaling the reading of the students' notes for raw tedium.

But a discernible change had come over the trial. Christie, for the most part, seemed to recede into the background and Keegstra, in control, turned the courtroom into a classroom. He was a teacher once more, projecting his fervor and self-assurance at the jury and out to the spectators. His hands worked expressively and his voice underscored the significance of his major points. The writings may have been important tools of the defence, but to Keegstra, they were touchstones. He would use them as platforms to launch himself into elaborate answers which left Christie and his questions far behind.

The written material fell into two categories: conspiracy literature which Keegstra had obtained from friends and from the Canadian Intelligence Service; and books not directly related to the conspiracy, but which reinforced his theory. They included conventional history books, obscure writings by so-called insiders who knew the truth about the Hidden Hand and works by Jewish authors who Keegstra said were exposing the activities of their co-religionists, either out of conscience or inadvertently.

Keegstra set great stock in anything written by the famous or near famous. He often quoted a passage from a fictional work by Benjamin Disraeli, the Jewish-born prime minister of Victorian England, as saying Jews were like moles burrowing under the foundations of European society. Abraham Lincoln, said Keegstra, feared the conspirators behind him in Washington more than the Confederate Army in front of him during the American Civil War. Even Karl Marx, whom Keegstra considered part of the conspiracy, was plumbed for evidence that capitalism was the spirit of Jewry. Despite Marx's leanings,

Keegstra said, the father of communism wrote some things he could agree with.

One of the best-known sources was Winston Churchill. Keegstra used a 1920 article written by the future British prime minister for a London weekly newspaper to show his students that statesmen were well aware of the conspiracy and its origins. The article, entitled "Zionism Versus Bolshevism, a Struggle for the Soul of the Jewish People," suggested there were good "national" Jews who were loyal to their countries. "International Jews" who had forsaken the "faith of their forefathers" had been responsible for revolutionary upheavals since the French Revolution. The thread ran from Spartacus (Adam) Weishaupt, founder of the Illuminati, to the modern Bolsheviks, whose top leaders, excluding Lenin, were atheistic Jews, Churchill wrote.

Keegstra found some areas of disagreement with Churchill. He would not accept Churchill's assertion that Christianity owes it ethical foundations to Judaism or that the "international" Jews had become revolutionaries because their people had suffered persecution. Keegstra also differed with the article's main premise: that Zionism was a bulwark against Bolshevism, giving Jews a sense of identity and pride and that it should be British policy to foster Zionism and live up to the 1917 Balfour Declaration, which said the British government "looks with favor" on the idea of a Jewish homeland in Palestine. Zionism and Bolshevism, to Keegstra, were different faces of the same conspiracy.

Another important work was Alfred Lilienthal's *The Zionist Connection*. Lilienthal, a Jewish American, was an ardent anti-Zionist who believed American Jews should owe their allegiance to the United States alone and not divide their loyalties between America and Israel. Keegstra said Lilienthal was a Jew exposing the illegitimacy of the state of Israel by writing that Jews had confused having a homeland with having a state, and mixed up religion with political nationalism. The book also supported the reasoning behind the true-false question which asked students whether or not Jews generally were good citizens and required an answer of false.

Economic historian Anthony Sutton's works on U.S. economic support of the Soviet Union fit in with Keegstra's view that the conspirators manipulated the policies of both governments to ensure the survival of the Jewish-dominated Communist regime.

Keegstra considered mainstream works untrustworthy and took the meat of his theory from tracts by "independent researchers," writers he said were interested more in revealing the truth than in making names for themselves.

Nesta Webster was at the top of his list, he said. Lauded by the likes of Churchill and H. G. Wells, Webster drew the connection between the Jewish conspiracy and the calamities of history since the French Revolution. The daughter of a British clergyman, Webster's research was so deep she imagined that her insights into the deeds of the Jacobins of the French Revolution—she and Keegstra believed them to be Jewish-led—came from her belief she was possessed by the spirit of a French countess of the era. That admission didn't trouble Keegstra, who said her research spoke for itself.

*Facts are Facts*, a diatribe against the Talmud in the form of an open letter from a Jew named Benjamin Freedman, formed the basis of classroom lectures about the sinister aspects of Judaism. Students were given copies of the work and told to write essays about it. Keegstra used other material, including an analysis of the Talmud by a writer named Elizabeth Dilling and a work by Martin Luther, who besides being one of the main figures in the Protestant Reformation also wrote anti-Jewish tracts when the Jews refused to convert to Christianity.

The readings from the witness stand covered every aspect of Keegstra's theory, and the subjects were as diverse as 2,000 years of history and philosophy could make them.

Much of the material came to Keegstra from the Canadian Intelligence Service, an arm of the Canadian League of Rights, and its international affiliates in the United States and Europe. Keegstra had been on the group's mailing list since the late 1960s and its monthly newsletter and bi-weekly bulletins gave him the real story behind current events, he said. There was nothing happening in the news—save perhaps isolated acts of God—that did not bear scrutiny from the conspiracy perspective.

For example, the Watergate scandal, which forced the resignation of U.S. president Richard Nixon in 1974, was engineered by the conspirators because Nixon had exposed Communists in the U.S. State Department, beginning in 1949. Nixon's advisors, who were members of the conspiracy, advised him to put the secret tape-recording system into the White House so he would ultimately incriminate himself, Keegstra reasoned.

For someone with a degree in education, supposedly versed in historical research, Keegstra seemed to have trouble reading the material he relied upon so heavily. For example, *ambivalence* came out *ambi-violence*. *Leviathan* became *levathen* and *megalomania* was *megamania*. Foreign or foreign-sounding words seemed to cause the most trouble. He pronounced the French philosopher *Proudhon* as *Proud-hawn*, *Machiavelli* became *Macavalley* and the *Marquis de Sade* the *Marquess de Sadie*. The African country of *Zimbabwe* repeatedly came out *Zimbowie*. Clearly embarrassed, Keegstra said he had trouble pronouncing words because he did not take "phonics"—phonetics—in school, as children do today.

But if Keegstra kept tripping over the big words, he understood the big message. The central theme, the conspiracy, remained front and centre through 19 days of direct examination by Christie. Canadians were supporting the Zionist conspiracy by buying Israeli national bonds, Keegstra said at one point. They even had the support of Prime Minister Brian Mulroney, who happened to have attended a bond dinner in Montreal the previous evening.

There was evidence that former Canadian prime minister Joe Clark supported the conspiracy's one-world government plans, Keegstra said. The proof? A letter Clark had sent to a Keegstra acquaintance supporting a greater sharing of Canada's wealth with poorer nations.

Reaction to the hours of fantastic theorizing varied with the listener. Reporters who covered the trial from the beginning became numb to the blithe discussions of Jewish atrocities and treachery, often taking the edge off what they heard with black humor. To them the trial had developed a Twilight Zone air early on.

A staunch core of Keegstra supporters, about a dozen all told, sat quietly or nodded knowingly at his testimony. Some passed the time reading from Bibles or other books. Lorraine Keegstra, who favored red and was always well groomed, generally sat in the front row of the gallery behind her husband, displaying the same sort of good-humored stoicism Keegstra himself showed to the public.

Each day, a new group of casual spectators, including young Jews from B'nai B'rith camps in the lake country around Red Deer, and school field trips from the city itself, became initiated to the fraternity. Few stayed more than a couple of hours. It had become a kind of side show which required an obligatory peek, but no more, lest the interest be considered perverse.

It was hardest for the Jews who came to see for themselves. Some gaped, shocked at what they were hearing. The Jewish children looked puzzled and disturbed by what they heard. During a recess, one reporter observed a group of three or four pre-teens start reflexively as Keegstra walked by and flashed them a smile. Manuel Prutschi, observer for the Canadian Jewish Congress, was spotted in the foyer one day, his head in his hands. What's the matter, he was asked, can't you take it? "No," the dazed Prutschi replied. "Sometimes I can't." Another Jewish man, a Red Deer resident, took to baiting Keegstra and his supporters with insults during breaks.

Little wonder. Keegstra told the court his "research" produced evidence that the Talmud condoned sex with young girls, sex with the dead—which Keegstra misnamed pederasty—that it sanctioned the murder of Christians and allowed Jews to break vows to non-Jews. It was, he concluded, "a book that promotes evil acts and teaches immoral things." The Talmud sprang from the ideology of the Pharisees, a Hebrew sect who Keegstra said had been condemned for abandoning the law of God.

"They were rationalizing evils which the Scriptures could never, would never rationalize. It really supported the truth of what I have been saying."

The Jews, said Keegstra, kept the truth of the Talmud secret. Since the Talmud is evil, the conspiracy based on it must also be secret. The international financiers worked behind the scenes to get control of national economies and put countries in debt. They had secretive organizations such as the Bilderbergers, the Trilateral Commission and the U.S. Council on Foreign Relations to co-ordinate their plans, but no outsiders ever knew what went on at their meetings.

"Men who have to do things in secret must have some evil plan," Keegstra concluded.

As each day passed, with an average three and a half hours of testimony a day, Keegstra showed no signs of backing away from the anti-Jewish material contained in his students' notes. On the contrary, he embraced it. Christie, at the beginning of direct examination, had Keegstra assess the accuracy of the passages from Trudi Roth's notes which Fraser had highlighted. Keegstra repeatedly endorsed them, saying that some qualifying words and class discussion might be missing, but otherwise they contained the essence of what he had taught. Christie's earlier efforts, aimed at making the notes seem unreliable reflections of his client's teaching, went for nought.

One point was hammered home. Keegstra had stressed that the conspiracy encompassed only five or six per cent of all Jews, including the revolutionaries and financiers. He said that's why he didn't insist on precision in the notes or essays when referring to Jews.

"Because it was understood, I did not demand they put in qualifying words. They understood it, at least most of them did, had they been listening. When I was teaching I never once thought this type of thing would come up and be under the scrutiny of exactness."

Some students inevitably misunderstood, said Keegstra. Blair Andrew, son of his nemesis Marg Andrew, was profligate in his use of the term "gutter rats," referring to all Jews when Keegstra had meant for it to mean Bolshevik-Jewish revolutionaries. He had had to threaten Blair with punishment if he didn't stop, said Keegstra.

The conspirators would ruthlessly use the "little Jew" to meet their ends, but he hadn't meant to indict the whole Jewish people as a party to the plot, Keegstra said. Nevertheless, there were some disturbing qualifications. For instance, Keegstra said the Jews of Europe who ended up in Nazi concentration camps were not totally innocent. World Jewry had declared war on Hitler in 1933 and again in 1939, forcing Hitler to treat Jews as potential saboteurs, he said.

"The Zionists cannot say the Jew is an innocent victim being put in concentration camps," said Keegstra.

Keegstra's direct testimony ended with a flourish. What, asked Christie, was the most important single source of your beliefs? The Bible, Keegstra responded. Christie produced one and asked that it be marked as the final defence exhibit.

Rehashing his interpretation of Christ's teaching in a sermon-like manner, Keegstra said he believed in the Bible, which taught that those who believe they are a chosen people are following not God's law, but a law of their own. The Bible is the antithesis of the Talmud's atheistical, materialist philosophy, he said. If one obeyed the Bible's call to love thy neighbor, "you're not going to go out and shoot him . . . starve him . . . try to dominate him."

Christians are obliged to rebuke their neighbors if they spy them sinning, said Keegstra, harkening back to his puzzlement at being attacked for merely telling the truth about the evils of Judaism. The Bible preaches truth, while those who believe in the conspiracy favor secrecy.

Compared to the almost languid pace of direct examination, the prosecution's cross-examination was short and brisk, lasting only seven days. It might have gone longer but for a ruling by MacKenzie preventing Fraser from putting questions to Keegstra from any material the accused couldn't identify.

Even before Fraser could begin, Christie found it an opportune time to move for a mistrial, his client having had his say. Once again he told MacKenzie media coverage of the trial had simply been too prejudicial to guarantee a just verdict. He cited several examples: an article in the local paper, a letter to *Alberta Report* magazine, an Edmonton television newscast—seen in Red Deer—in which an announcer connected Nazi war criminal Joseph Mengele, whose bones had just been found in South America, to Keegstra's views on the Holocaust in a transition between the two news items, and finally a magazine article published in April.

MacKenzie handled this application the same way he had dealt with Christie's other protests about trial coverage and pre-trial publicity. The Canadian system of justice gives some credit to the intelligence of the jurors, provided they are properly charged to ignore everything but the evidence they hear in court. The application was dismissed.

The relationship between Fraser and Keegstra was set at the beginning.

"Who does this gentleman who is about to cross-examine me represent?" Keegstra asked MacKenzie.

"This gentleman represents the Crown as you well know, Mr. Keegstra," said the judge with a hint of impatience.

Fraser began his questioning by saying Keegstra had referred to himself as a historian, although not fully fledged. What are your qualifications? Do you hold a degree in history?

"I do not," replied Keegstra. "Don't forget, to be a teacher you don't have to have those."

"I'm not interested in anything you have to tell me except to answer my questions," Fraser said sharply. The stage was set.

Keegstra insisted he had done as thorough a job as possible researching the material he taught his students, considering the workload he had and the limited resources available. He attended a seminar on social studies and discussed his views with "so-called historians," not one of whom rebutted him. Why do you think mainstream historians and their books don't mention the conspiracy? asked Fraser.

"They're all under the control of what I'm going to say are the conspirators," Keegstra replied.

Conventional historians, he said, are afraid of losing writing contracts, prestige and revenue by revealing the truth. So he had to rely on "independent researchers" he could trust, such as the Canadian Intelligence Service and Nesta Webster.

"We're in a power struggle here. We're not playing tiddlywinks."

His students, said Keegstra, had to be told the truth. Social studies was under the control of the conspiracy, which was trying to indoctrinate their young minds with secular humanism.

Keegstra said he taught a more balanced view of history than was available from the censored social studies text. Students were at liberty to disagree, and he urged them to discuss it with parents and other teachers.

The exchanges were beginning to animate Keegstra's followers in the gallery, packed for the first day of cross-examination. They muttered at Fraser's questions and laughed at and applauded Keegstra's ripostes. After a few minutes, MacKenzie had had enough.

"I'm not putting up with that kind of nonsense at all," he growled. "I'm not going to have those kinds of outbursts. The jury is carrying too big a burden. If you want to be entertained, go find a movie theatre."

The last straw had been a question by Fraser about Keegstra's claim to spiritual support for his beliefs. Keegstra had been referring to himself as "we" ever since taking the stand. At first it was taken to mean Keegstra and his pupils were in agreement on his theory, but he later explained to Christie he believed that if he was speaking the truth the Holy Spirit would be with him in the classroom.

"If I believe in Christ, he will send a comforter," Keegstra would reiterate to Fraser in cross-examination. "Ought we not to acknowledge that fact? I don't want to be I. I has that sound of egotism, selfishness."

While laying in wait for Keegstra, Fraser and Phillippe had been taking notes during Christie's examination, ordering transcripts of testimony for certain days. Now it was put to use.

Fraser quizzed Keegstra about his Calvinist background and asked if he was aware that John Calvin had converted from Judaism and that his original name was Cohen. He had heard that, Keegstra responded, but it wouldn't matter if it was true since Calvin agreed with the Scriptures.

But you said anyone who changes his name must have something to hide and possibly be evil, Fraser said, referring to Keegstra's condemnation of men who used pseudonyms, such as Trotsky, Stalin and Spartacus Weishaupt.

"There has to be a reason for aliases," said Keegstra. Maybe it was an innocent name change to signify his acceptance of Christianity.

If Calvin changed his name, was he part of the conspiracy?

Keegstra couldn't say.

Fraser recalled from Keegstra's testimony that he'd taught students that Jews were reluctant to become German citizens, making the Nazis wary of them. Correct, said Keegstra. Hitler also decreed that foreigners couldn't own property in Germany, he said.

Didn't you know the Nazi party platform forbade Jews from becoming citizens?

Well, said Keegstra, he knew people who knew Jews who maintained their German citizenship and whose businesses stayed open through the war.

You handed out the Nazi party platform to your students, Fraser pressed on. Did you fail to draw attention to the Jewish restrictions because they didn't support your view? False, said Keegstra. The students had the entire platform in the handout. He didn't discuss all the planks in the interests of time.

The needling quality of Fraser's questions put Keegstra on the defensive. Confronted with the debate he had often asked for from opponents, he adopted a sneering tone in his responses.

"You agree the notes reflect your teaching?" asked Fraser.

"Roughly," said Keegstra. There could have been some mistakes, deletions or additions. In any case, he wasn't responsible for how his students interpreted the lectures.

"If they're the closest thing you've got, you haven't got much," he said.

Fraser turned to Keegstra's scholastic record, especially his work in obtaining a Bachelor of Education degree. Keegstra did well at courses on how to teach industrial arts, scoring honors. But on the two history courses he did less well, earning 64 per cent in Canadian history and 57 per cent in European history. Keegstra said that he really only got interested in history after he completed the teaching degree and that he had more faith in home study anyway, because it took place away from the corrupting influence of universities.

Keegstra's cross-examination brought his personal view of Jews into finer focus. Jews, he said, were damned to perdition because they had rejected Christ. Christ himself had said they were of the devil.

"That's not my definition. That's what the Scriptures say and I believe the Scriptures."

Those who don't believe in Christ can still have a spark of good in them, but that won't save them come Judgment Day, he said.

"That's why they [the Jews] had the hatred towards Christianity," he said.

Did being pro-Christian, as Keegstra described himself, mean the same as being anti-Jewish? Fraser asked.

"I'm not going to say," said Keegstra. "I'll put it to you this way. A Jew is very anti-Christian and if that makes a Christian anti-Jewish, then a Christian is anti-Jewish. I am against their philosophy and their religion because they are so vehemently against mine. I have to be anti anything that's hatred."

Fraser reminded Keegstra of a diagram which appeared in many of the students' notes. Keegstra had sketched out two world views, one governed by God, the other by man-made faiths. The first included Christianity; the other described the evils of evolution, secular humanism and socialism, which Keegstra later told his students were the products of Judaism.

By presenting students with this life-and-death choice, between Christian salvation and eternal damnation, wasn't Keegstra using the very techniques of the Big Fear which he accused the conspiracy of employing?

"The fear of God is the beginning of wisdom," Keegstra explained, adding that a little fear was not harmful if it led students to follow a better way of life.

You don't like these people who are out to destroy your religion, do you? asked Fraser.

"That's right," said Keegstra, quickly adding, "I would have more dislike for their actions, for what they are trying to do to me."

You would find these people extremely detestable, Fraser suggested.

"I do, and why ought I not to have that?" Keegstra said.

And you would pass this on to your students? said Fraser.

"That would be right."

Keegstra said he warned his pupils to be wary of all Jews, lest they were part of the small proportion involved in the conspiracy. There was no way of telling who was in the plot just by looking at them. One had to look at their actions.

"Nevertheless, we do not have to observe and watch, and as co-religionists they do work well together," he said.

Despite a ruling by MacKenzie forbidding Fraser from questioning Keegstra about material he didn't recognize, the prosecutor was able to suggest Keegstra hadn't done much research on the Talmud.

He admitted he hadn't read any works on the Talmud other than Dilling, Freedman and an obscure Russian Roman Catholic priest who lived in czarist St. Petersburg. He felt he didn't need help to understand its true meaning. If he relied on a Talmud scholar he would just wind up interpreting it the way the author intended, said Keegstra.

"When they state it so plainly, does it need an interpretation?" Keegstra asked.

Through questions, Fraser learned Keegstra didn't know the

origin of the concept of the Talmud, what schools of interpretation existed, how it was divided, exactly where and when it was written or the background of the contributors.

To Christie, all this sounded like Fraser was trying to sneak his material into evidence. If the Crown wanted to call a Talmud expert to the stand he would relish cross-examining one, he said.

But MacKenzie allowed the questions, noting he'd already told the jury the contents of Fraser's questions, with their references to books and authors Keegstra didn't know about, weren't evidence. Keegstra's answers were.

Fraser harkened back to Keegstra's opinion that the Talmud allowed Jews to break vows to non-Jews. Did Keegstra know what the word vow meant in the context of the Talmud? he asked. Keegstra said he assumed it would be the common use of the word. Had he bothered to look up vow in the standard Jewish encyclopedia? No, said Keegstra, it wasn't important.

"I thought when they put down the word vow, that's what it meant. If they are going to use a word, let it mean what it means. It ought to mean one thing and one thing only."

Fraser succeeded in getting several volumes of the Talmud thrown out as defence exhibits after Keegstra admitted he hadn't actually read them during his research. The first time he'd seen them was in preparation for the case. He had told Christie earlier he had used the volumes to check Talmud extracts in Dilling's book. Now he told Fraser he had actually asked a friend in Edmonton to go to the university library and check them for him. He had taken the friend's word they matched.

Having defined Keegstra's views on Jews and Judaism, Fraser went to work on his historical sources.

Keegstra, he suggested, found it convenient to include material which confirmed his ideas, even if he wasn't familiar with the source.

Had he, Fraser asked, inquired into the background of Ron Gostick and Patrick Walsh, the prime movers of the Canadian League of Rights and Canadian Intelligence Service?

They were Christians, said Keegstra, and Social Crediters. Gostick, in fact, was the son of a former Alberta Social Credit member of the legislature.

"I trusted Ron and Pat," said Keegstra. "They've been in my home. You have to trust people whether you like it or not."

What about their academic credentials? said Fraser. Gostick had no more than a high school education and Walsh, who billed himself as a former RCMP undercover agent, was simply a onetime police informant, said the prosecutor.

No matter, Keegstra shrugged. Academic titles were unimportant to him, perhaps even a liability. Someone with a string of degrees "could be nothing more than a dupe and lackey of the conspiracy, trained to regurgitate exactly what they desire him to regurgitate."

What about Nesta Webster, who was interested in the occult and linked to Britain's Fascist movement in the interwar years? asked Fraser. He pressed Keegstra to explain how he had checked her credentials, but Keegstra could produce little beyond the endorsements found on the jacket covers of her books. Still, he said, she did good research, as indicated by the lengthy bibliographies at the end of her works.

Was Keegstra familiar with the sources of much of the material he received from the League, that they originated with anti-Semitic groups in the United States? Keegstra said he wasn't familiar with the groups Fraser mentioned.

Keegstra also said he readily accepted an extract of a letter he received detailing Jewish involvement in the Bolshevik Revolution, sent by a member of the U.S. expeditionary force because it had official-looking archival stamps on it and despite the fact it had been mailed to him anonymously.

He also took at face value a book entitled *My Exploited Father-in-Law* by Curtis B. Dahl, about Jewish influence on U.S. president Franklin D. Roosevelt, despite the fact Dahl was divorced from Anna Roosevelt before FDR was elected president and was never a White House insider.

Fraser challenged Keegstra on the "Protocols of the Learned Elders of Zion," a document purported to be the master plan of the world Jewish conspiracy, worked out at a meeting in Switzerland. The work was widely denounced as a forgery soon after it was "discovered" in 1905, but Keegstra maintained that its authenticity had never been conclusively disproved. Besides, he told Fraser, even if it was a forgery, it had been very accurate about world events and causes behind them. It was an example of the circular logic which sustained Keegstra throughout his testimony.

Fraser now went after the contradictions in the sources themselves. He listed mainstream works on a variety of topics, from the Russian Revolution to the history of the Jews, which Keegstra said he had never read. Even if he did read them, Keegstra said, he would have to check the background of the authors to discern their biases.

Fraser had planned to use a number of books to challenge

many of Keegstra's assertions about history, but after repeated objections from Christie, MacKenzie ruled out material Keegstra had not identified or adopted.

Earlier, during Christie's direct examination, MacKenzie had not allowed the defence to enter books Keegstra might have read subsequent to his firing as post facto support of his conspiracy theory.

So Fraser turned to the contradictions in Keegstra's own books. For example, he suggested that Keegstra had ignored statements in a book condemning modern capitalism by American author Cleon Skousen which specifically warned the work should not be construed as alleging a Jewish conspiracy. Fraser asked if he had privileged the students with this disclaimer. Keegstra said he couldn't recall having done so, but in any case students had access to all kinds of other material countering the conspiracy theory.

Likewise, Anthony Sutton's work on the Soviet economy's reliance on Western support contained few references to Jews and none on a conspiracy.

"Here again, he gets all these facts and you have to make inferences," said Keegstra.

In one work about the relationship between the Bolsheviks and Wall Street, Sutton even denounced the conspiracy theory, said Fraser.

"I know you have tried to mislead me in some areas, so I'm not going to necessarily agree," Keegstra said. "I don't agree with any author completely. No one would agree with me completely and I don't think that's so terrible."

Did Keegstra bother to tell students that John D. Rockefeller, whom he had described to them as a Sephardic Jew from Portugal, was generally considered to be a Baptist?

"I think I told the students that he put himself out to be a Baptist," said Keegstra, but added that no real Baptist would have behaved the way ultra-capitalist Rockefeller did.

Fraser challenged Keegstra on what he taught students about the 1967 Arab-Israel War. The notes revealed that Keegstra told them the Soviets had collaborated with the Israelis in setting remote control bombs in Egyptian air force jets, which is why photos of Israeli air strikes show mostly direct hits on the planes. They also were told Israel captured most of Egypt's Soviet-built tanks intact in the desert because saboteurs had removed the rotors from ignition systems. Israeli troops, equipped with just those rotors, got the armor running in short order after Egyptian crews abandoned it. Keegstra admitted, though, that the stories about remote-controlled bombs and

*A destroyed Egyptian Air Force jet in the 1967 Six-Day Arab-Israeli War. Although he later admitted he had no evidence, Keegstra speculated that the apparently precise Israeli air attacks were due to remote-control bombs planted on the planes by Israel's Soviet collaborators—part of the worldwide Jewish conspiracy. (London Daily Express)*

missing ignition rotors were speculation on his part, based on his knowledge as a mechanic. Keegstra apparently wasn't aware that Soviet tanks, diesel-powered since the Second World War, don't require ignition rotors.

Keegstra interpreted a book on world capitalism entitled *Tragedy and Hope* as reinforcing his Jewish conspiracy theory despite only one reference to the term Jew in the 1,000-page work by a Professor Quigley.

"I suggest even if he doesn't want to say it, it's still there," said Keegstra.

Keegstra couldn't pin down precisely where he derived the percentage of the world's Jews who were involved in the conspiracy but under questioning from Fraser disclosed that this added up to a lot of Jews. If there were about 18 million Jews in the world, as census figures show, and up to eight per cent were involved in the conspiracy, that would add up to about 1.5 million, Keegstra agreed. But, said Fraser, you testified earlier Jews purposely fudge their true numbers on the low side and speculated there could be twice as many as official figures indicate. This, Fraser reminded him, was one of the ways you tried to account for the six million said to have died in the Holocaust. They were secretly slipped into other countries, such as the United States. If that's so, then the eight per cent would add up to three million or more conspirators, Fraser concluded. That's correct, said Keegstra.

Who are they? Other than the Rothschild banking family and a number of long-dead historical figures, Keegstra had trouble identifying the conspirators.

Keegstra disowned Jewish author Alfred Lilienthal, whom in earlier testimony he had flourished as a Jew who had blown the whistle on all-powerful Zionism. The Jews themselves admit what is going on, he would say.

But Fraser noted Lilienthal, in *The Zionist Connection*, condemned the Nazi genocide and stated anti-Semitism is a fact "no one but the irrational would deny."

"This is this man's opinion, again," Keegstra said. "He states a large number of facts that I could use. I'm saying to you, sometimes he draws irrational conclusions from the facts."

Keegstra rejected Lilienthal's list of Jews who had made vital contributions to the United States, from Einstein in science to Supreme Court Justice Felix Frankfurter, who to Keegstra was among the conspirators.

"I have seen a lot of detrimental things they have done to the American culture," he said.

Finally, Fraser brought back some of the student essays, with their derogatory descriptions of Jewish actions and dire warnings for the future.

Why, he asked, were students who didn't support this conspiracy theory given lower marks? Keegstra said the poorer marks were not because they offered the conventional view of history but because, as in Lorriene Bogdane's case, they plagiarized encyclopedias and didn't provide facts to back their arguments.

Even in essays which disagreed with his conspiracy theory, students were expected to include some of the points he considered important.

"If you don't put in the essays what was discussed in class, what was the sense of holding a class?" he asked.

He said he saw nothing wrong with describing as garbage and Zionist propaganda the material he questioned in student essays. Encyclopedias, after all, provided the conspiracy's censored view of history.

Yet essays which supported his views didn't need the rigorous documentation and earned fewer comments because "I knew the source because I lectured on it."

Keegstra offered a variety of answers to the question of why he hadn't commented on essays which suggested that Hitler was right to move against the Jews, that Jews should be destroyed and that "we have to get rid of every Jew in existence." For one, he couldn't possibly write detailed comments on all the essays in the limited time reserved for marking. He also did not want to discourage independent thinking among the students, especially those like Richard Denis who made that statement. Such students seemed indifferent to marks anyway.

Now Keegstra told Fraser he had left the papers' conclusions unremarked because he understood what they really meant to say and he agreed with them. The essays weren't advocating violence against Jews, he said. Since Jews were identified by religion, not race, and Keegstra wanted to convert them to Christianity, getting rid of Jews meant eradicating their false and evil religion, he said.

"If we replace that ideology with Christian ideology, then we will get rid of Jews with Christian thinking," Keegstra told Fraser.

Fraser ended his cross-examination, leaving Christie much to repair and little material to do it with. Re-examination lasted perhaps 20 minutes as MacKenzie sustained Fraser's frequent objections. Christie's questions, the judge said, did not relate to anything new brought up in cross-examination, but merely reiterated what Keegstra had said in previous testimony. Re-examination was meant to clarify evidence, not bolster it.

"That's the case for the defence, m'Lord," said Christie.

Christie's summation lasted 15 hours over three days. Despite weeks of testimony, much of it turgid, and the presentation of 266 exhibits the defence counsellor hadn't lost his sense of the dramatic. A guilty verdict, he said, would erode freedom in Canada. The jurors would play a role in determining the future freedoms in their country.

"Fear will grow and silence will grow and people will be more and more suspicious about what they say and who they say it to," if the jury returns a conviction, Christie said.

Christie ignored the Quigley pre-trial decision on the constitutionality of the law and told the jury freedom of expression is never an issue until it is lost.

The government, backed by powerful, unidentified forces, wants to suppress ideas it does not like and is using the court to do it, he said.

"They just want to shut him up and they want you to help them do it," he said. It was "a new McCarthyism of the left."

Christie, once again facing the jury and speaking in a voice shorn of any excess emotion, compared the Keegstra case to the Scopes Monkey Trial, which had begun 60 years ago that week. John Scopes, a teacher in Dayton, Tennessee, was tried and convicted for teaching Darwin's theory of evolution, forbidden under state law.

Keegstra, said Christie, had been subjected to an unprecedented smear campaign, condemned even by members of Parliament and the premier of the province, men who had never even met him.

"Mass murderers have not had so many bad things said about them," said Christie.

Keegstra's belief that Jews have a false, evil religion is based on his honest interpretation of Scripture, something allowed under the law, he said.

"Behind me sits an honest man. He has his faults, but dishonesty isn't one of them and neither is hate."

Christie attacked the Crown's case as "shifty," saying the indictment was cleverly worded to cover four years of teaching so it would be difficult to defend against a single act. While Fraser glowered silently, Christie said the prosecution did not specify particular statements as hateful because it knew there was evidence to the contrary. Instead, it selected a limited number of notebooks and essays from the hundreds of students Keegstra taught.

Only one student, Kelly Cordon, said there was hatred in the material and none said they acquired hatred from Keegstra's teachings. On the contrary, Christie said, most became more skeptical and thoughtful.

The law's statutory defence of discussion in good faith on a religious subject forces the jury to decide whether a religious belief is held sincerely, Christie said. Christianity is an uncompromising religion which forces its followers to make a clear choice based on faith.

"If you're a Christian, then Judaism is a false way," he said.

True Christians are obliged to tell the truth about their religion, which is what Keegstra did in class, said Christie.

If the law was to be applied to historical figures, Christ himself would be among the first to be charged for criticizing the Jews in the Bible, and Martin Luther indicted and his works banned because he wrote an anti-Jewish tract.

Keegstra never forced his views about Jews and the conspiracy on his students, said Christie. They were not a captive audience, and the fact that none of them said they acquired hatred should weigh in Keegstra's guilt or innocence.

The Crown, he said, pressured the student witnesses to twist

Keegstra's teaching, and news reports in the wake of Keegstra's firing had clouded their perceptions of what he taught.

The jury should analyse the notes which the Crown alleges are the written evidence of Keegstra's teachings.

The students were under pressure to relate everything to Jews. Stephen Lecerf seemed to feel he was expected to give certain answers and Paul Maddox admitted he'd been under pressure from the media, the prosecution and his mother, Christie said.

"The notes are inaccurate in every respect, naturally, and you can't take them as gospel truth of anything," said Christie.

True, the Crown found similarities among the 20 sets of notes entered as evidence, but there were many more contradictions which bring their accuracy into question, he said.

Keegstra may have been selective in teaching his theory, but no more so than other teachers, said Christie. Dick Hoeksema admitted he gave students his opinions but never backed them up. But Hoeksema was "on the side of the angels," and so would not be charged with doing basically what Keegstra had done.

Christie wove the freedom of speech argument through his assessment of the evidence and frequently guessed at what the Crown would say in summation.

By late Thursday afternoon, the second day of Christie's argument, Fraser took the opportunity during the jury's absence for a recess, to raise an objection. Christie, he said, had said a number of things to the jury which he shouldn't. He had referred to the possibility of a jail term. The penalty shouldn't weigh in the jury's deliberations. He had made a passing reference to a newspaper article about the trial when the judge had ordered jurors to ignore news coverage. He had read them case law, which is MacKenzie's prerogative, and he had made statements about the merits of the legislation (the freedom of speech argument), about the prosecution's motives in the case, and about statements by Premier Peter Lougheed which weren't before the court.

Christie countered he had a right to comment on the merits of the legislation. The premier's statements were "public knowledge," and as for the publicity, he was trying to help the jury disregard it and put news reports into perspective by raising an example of distorted reporting.

But MacKenzie was unimpressed. He said Christie was raising some things at the peril of the whole proceeding, "which in this particular case would be nothing short of tragedy."

Christie didn't discard the freedom argument completely,

though. It became an integral part of his dissertation on the defence of allowing statements "relevant to any subject of public interest, the discussion of which is for the public benefit, and if on reasonable grounds, he believed them to be true."

The jury must decide, he said, whether the broadest discussion of views, no matter how unpopular, was not in the public interest.

For Keegstra, the conflict between Christianity and Judaism was ideological warfare—"Christ versus anti-Christ."

"If you don't believe what I say, please read the Bible when you consider the evidence," Christie told the jury.

He attacked the Crown's evidence, saying the students who took hateful inferences from Keegstra's teachings—such as Cordon, Bogdane and Maddox—bore grudges against him, were irresponsible, or were encouraged by their parents to relate everything he taught to Jews. But it was obvious that others, such as Ramstead and Matthews, were honest, pleasant young people who admitted they couldn't remember everything Keegstra might have said and agreed their notes weren't completely accurate.

Christie asked the jury to think of Matthews, polite, friendly, coping with her disability. She offered no evidence of bitterness, save for her wish to see drunken drivers banished from her concept of an ideal society.

"If this is a product of Jim Keegstra's teaching, then where was there evidence of hate?" he asked.

Keegstra, on the stand, displayed the sincerity and devotion to principles which should convince the jury he could never wilfully promote hatred, said Christie.

The only time Keegstra ever knowingly met a Jew, Bob Epstein, he opened his home to him because he was down on his luck and gave him bus fare back to his home in the United States, said Christie.

"If this is a man who hates Jews, why would he treat anyone like that who was a Jew? The truth of the matter is there's evidence of goodwill."

The prosecution was a waste of time, money and effort, he said.

In a wrap-up that included allusions to martyrdom and heavenly support for his client, Christie said no matter what the verdict, Keegstra had been morally acquitted.

"If you acquit Jim Keegstra, you make him what he really is, an innocent man," he said. "If you convict him . . . you will condemn him, not as a criminal, but as a man who stands by his beliefs."

Fraser, naturally, begged to differ.

The Crown, he said, at the beginning of a three-and-a-half-hour summation, felt satisfied it had proven its case through the students' notes and essays, but Keegstra's 26 days on the stand had amounted to a "confession under oath."

"Through the process of direct examination and cross-examination, he has proved the charge . . . through his own mouth."

Fraser had been fuming at Christie's attacks on the Crown's motives and tactics. Now, he lashed back. The defence lawyer had used scare tactics and political speech making in his final argument to try to distract the jury from the fact he had no real defence, said the prosecutor. Christie's arguments amounted to "wilful blindness."

Christie's freedom of speech argument, which put the onus on the jury to preserve freedom in Canada, was nothing but a red herring, he said. Jury verdicts don't affect other cases. Only judicial decisions in higher courts can set legal precedents.

"Defence counsel knows this. He again tried to mislead you. Freedom of speech is not an issue for you to consider. I can't state that strongly enough. Your decision will have no effect on your children, as you were told. It will have no effect on anyone but the accused. This is simply a scare tactic."

Having slammed Christie, Fraser turned his attention to Keegstra. The former teacher was not the honest Christian he set himself up to be. He had purposely tried to mislead the jury with inconsistencies in his testimony, Fraser said, referring to the withdrawal of the Talmud exhibit which Keegstra admitted he hadn't really read and another book Keegstra conceded, when questioned, played no part in forming his opinion.

"I'll call them that to be kind," Fraser said. "I suggest he deliberately misled the court, deliberately.

"I suggest the credibility of the accused is very dubious."

The Crown didn't set out to find the words "I hate Jews" in the students' notes, but to illustrate that all of Keegstra's teaching added up to wilful hate promotion. Keegstra never used the word hatred directly in reference to the Jews, but during the testimony he said he had an intense dislike, detestation and abhorrence for people who did evil—all dictionary synonyms for hate.

The term "Jew" was always linked to negative events and evil men. Keegstra testified he had never heard anything good about Jews. Students were given a choice of two world views, between goodness and Christianity or evil and barbarism, with which Judaism was connected, said Fraser.

The conspiracy theory was a useful tool to promote hate,

Fraser said. Keegstra said only a small percentage of Jews were in the conspiracy, but he could not identify more than a few bankers, such as the Rothschilds, thus casting a shadow over all Jews.

"It was a convenient vehicle to allow the accused to blame everything on the Jews."

Keegstra's condemnation of the Talmud tarred almost all Jews by definition, since all but a tiny minority of Jews accept the Talmud as an article of their faith.

Keegstra had a captive audience, despite the defence's assertion to the contrary, said Fraser. Students were made to learn the material in order to repeat it in essays and tests. Those who did not received lower marks. Students testified Keegstra's course was easy to pass if you gave him what he wanted. Keegstra never provided students with the tools with which to challenge his theory, arguing they had access to alternative viewpoints outside his class.

And he lent the teachings spiritual authority by invoking Scripture, said Fraser.

Promotion was wilful because Keegstra must have known, or at least guessed, the results of his teaching.

Fraser tore into the statutory defences, arguing that only the defence of statements made for the public benefit had any relevance and that those statements required evidence of reasonable grounds. Keegstra's dubious sources didn't provide that defence. In fact, he chose to ignore or denigrate material in his sources when it didn't fit his theory. The approach is "not only unreasonable, it is irrational," Fraser said.

The religious defence does not stand up because condemning Judaism as an evil religion goes further than the statutory defence should allow, he said. Keegstra also displayed his ignorance of the religion on the stand, though he taught his opinions as if they were fact.

Keegstra is a hatemonger, Fraser said. He thrived on media attention despite complaints by his counsel.

"Does he look dejected?" Fraser asked the jury. "He's in his element. This is the high point in his life. Hatemongers thrive on publicity. They don't want this trial to end. It will be like taking his platform away from him."

Keegstra had been able to make his views known for 26 days, in spite of defence claims that the prosecution was aimed at shutting him up. "If that's so, we've done a poor job of it."

Now, after a fair trial, he would have to answer for his views.

"He must finally face up to what he has done and that time is near."

As Fraser had predicted, MacKenzie began his charge to the jury the following morning by telling it to ignore much of what Christie had said about freedom of speech.

"I can tell you as a matter of law that this legislation does not violate the Charter of Rights," he said, without referring directly to the Quigley decision.

The law against wilful hate promotion exists, and only Parliament can alter it. The jury has no right to pass judgment on its merits as a good or bad piece of legislation.

"For a juror to do that would be a violation of his or her oath," said the judge. "These are political arguments and have no place in a court of law."

The jury must be sure beyond a reasonable doubt that the Crown has proven the essential elements of wilfullness, hatred and promotion, as well as that the target was the Jewish people, an identifiable group under the law.

The wilfullness was crucial since the jury must be sure Keegstra intended to promote hatred in his teachings. "A crime cannot be committed accidentally," MacKenzie said.

The judge carefully reviewed the law and outlined the four statutory defences, explaining what was meant by "reasonable grounds" and "good faith."

MacKenzie said there was little in the evidence to support the statute's truth defence, but he surprised prosecutors when he suggested the fourth defence, that of making statements to remove hatred, might apply since the defence referred briefly to Keegstra's effort to balance the books on Jewish-inspired hatred of Arabs, Germans and Christians.

If the jury decides any one of the elements of the indictment was not proven or that any one of the defences applied, then it had to acquit Keegstra, MacKenzie said.

MacKenzie told the jurors not to be concerned about outside opinions.

"An acquittal of the accused cannot be taken as approval of, or agreement with, his actions, beliefs or teachings," he said.

As the jury filed out, moving down a back hallway to a larger jury room and unused courtroom at the other end of the building, Lorraine Keegstra cried quietly in the front row of the spectators' gallery. She had sat stoically through almost every day of the trial, noticeably absent during Fraser's biting cross-examination. Now the strain of more than 14 weeks, more than two years, for that matter, began to show. Keegstra, looking dazed and somewhat lost, wandered out of the courtroom while his wife was comforted by a friend.

It would take 30 hours to reach a verdict. The jury deliberated for the rest of the day after MacKenzie's charges, adjourning in the early evening to a hotel four blocks away, shepherded by the court clerk and a security escort. The same hotel was home for most reporters and Fraser. The close proximity would eventually get to Christie, who became upset that jurors were being photographed entering and leaving the courthouse and at breakfast in an isolated section of the hotel's restaurant. Although their names were on public record, Christie argued to MacKenzie the media "harassment" would make their faces known, especially to neighbors, perhaps prejudicing their ability to reach an impartial decision. MacKenzie ordered the cameramen to stay away from the jury.

A few hours after being sequestered, the jury returned for further clarification of the meaning of "reasonable grounds" and "good faith." MacKenzie simply amplified what he had said in his charge. Reasonable grounds involve what a reasonable person might use to form a belief under the same circumstances as the accused, that is, with the knowledge he had at his disposal. Good faith is concerned with the way a person acts. To act in good faith, the accused must hold an honest belief throughout, so Keegstra's sincerity played an important role.

The requests for information on the aspects of the statutory defences left some observers wondering whether the jury had already finished looking at the indictment and now was studying to see whether the defence applied. But it would be two and a half more days before anything happened.

Late Saturday morning, Christie had just finished protesting to MacKenzie that he had learned Fraser had eaten breakfast with reporters and an observer from the B'nai B'rith at the hotel restaurant, in view of the jury. Nothing of the sort had happened, Fraser said angrily.

"You might have asked your learned friend where he had breakfast this morning," said MacKenzie. "I'm sure in honesty he would have told you."

Christie and Keegstra had returned to the group's northwest Red Deer headquarters and were just sitting down to lunch when the call came at 1 p.m. A decision had been reached.

The courtroom was half empty as the jury filed in and took their seats. The faithful were scattered in the rows behind the defence table, the curious behind the three rows of reporters.

At 1:25 p.m., after calling the roll, court clerk Ingrid Ladouceur asked if a verdict had been reached. Foreman Dwight Arthur, a 26-year-old graphic artist from Red Deer, rose and read from a slip of paper: Guilty.

Behind the reporters a woman muttered, "Good."

# 10
# What Price Martyrdom?

---

*The object of punishment is, prevention from evil, it cannot be made impulsive to good.*

—Horace Mann

---

Fraser, after a short recess, asked MacKenzie to impose the maximum sentence under the law—two years in prison. The crime, he said, had been committed under the worst possible circumstances.

"The offence was conducted in the forum of a classroom," said the prosecutor. "The accused . . . had a position of trust."

By his own account, Keegstra taught perhaps 300 students during the period covered by the indictment.

"The position he had in that school he took advantage of for his own purposes," said Fraser.

The crime was not only committed against the Jewish people, but also Eckville, the people of Alberta and the Christian community in general. Moreover, Keegstra showed absolutely no signs of remorse.

"Rehabilitation is a long way down the road in this case," Fraser said. The sentence must be long and strong enough to deter the accused and others who hold the same views and wish to promote them.

Noting that Ernst Zundel was sentenced to 15 months in jail for distributing a pamphlet which people chose to read or ignore, Fraser said Keegstra's case was different—he had a captive audience.

Christie's pre-sentence argument could have stressed Keegstra's heart condition, or the fact that it was a non-violent crime or that it was the first offence of an otherwise reputable member of his community. Instead, the lawyer wrapped up in less than a minute and mentioned none of those things.

Keegstra, he said, spoke the truth according to his sincere beliefs.

"The accused stands before you with a clear conscience."

After another break, an hour after the jury's verdict, MacKenzie passed sentence.

The hate promotion legislation must be put into perspective with the rest of the Canadian Criminal Code, he said. The least serious indictable offences are those which carry maximum penalties of two years or less. The rationale for the sentence has to be considered. Jail terms are usually reserved for repeated offences. In the case of a first offence the court looks at alternatives—such as probation—when there is a real chance the guilty party will accept rehabilitation assistance. That prospect wasn't likely in this case, he said.

MacKenzie said that in committing the "serious" crime Keegstra disseminated slanderous ideas about the Jewish community. Most of the stories have been around for centuries and peaked with the barbarism of Nazi Germany. Keegstra's fanaticism "may present a menace to other people."

On the other hand, said MacKenzie, a lot of evidence had been presented indicating Keegstra's good character and stature in the town of Eckville.

"In many ways, this particular accused has in my view given decent service in his community and achieved a reputation of being faithful to his Christian convictions."

Keegstra's obsession with the conspiracy made him like a drug addict who also pushed drugs to survive, said MacKenzie. He was "as much a victim of the crime as perpetrator."

There was no punishment the court could impose which would rehabilitate Keegstra. The most serious punishment had already been delivered when he lost his privilege to teach.

"He has been deprived of doing something he truly loved doing," said the judge.

Yet society must show its revulsion at the promotion of hatred, he said.

Keegstra was fined $5,000.

MacKenzie also ordered that the books entered as defence evidence be turned over to the Attorney General's Department for disposal, all save the Bible which had been the defence's last exhibit. Christie asked for, and received, a month to pay the fine.

The denouement was unexpected. The hate promotion statute makes no reference to a fine, but the Canadian Criminal Code gives the courts the option of imposing fines for any offences where the maximum penalty is less than five years in prison.

Minutes later, Christie, followed by Keegstra, walked through the milling crowd of spectators and reporters, down the stairs, across the tiled foyer to the big main doors of the courthouse.

Frank Cottingham, publicity director of the Christian Defence League, half-skipped to keep up with Christie, who was marching, back straight, eyes front, towards the throng of reporters waiting outside. Cottingham had hold of Christie's elbow, his face shining in a state approaching bliss. For Keegstra's hardcore supporters, this was an outcome devoutly to be wished. The guilty verdict confirmed Keegstra's martyrdom for the just cause, even if the sentence decreed this could only be a crucifixion of the pocketbook.

Outside, a swarm of reporters and cameramen surrounded Keegstra.

"Well," he said, "the black cloud of fear and terror has descended on Canada. This is a defeat for all Canadians."

Did he feel he was punished lightly?

No. In a free society he should not have been penalized at all.

Would he appeal?

"Of course."

Back in the courthouse, Jim Green, leader of the Christian Defence League and a long-time Social Credit crony of Keegstra's, contemplated the prospect of raising money to pay the fine. The defence fund might not have enough in it to cover all the legal costs and the fine.

But Green could look for help from an unexpected quarter.

Nearby, jury foreman Dwight Arthur, who had remained in the courtroom to hear the sentence, said he was happy Keegstra had not gone to jail.

"If they establish a fund to help pay the fine, I will be contributing to it," said Arthur, who described himself as a Christian fundamentalist.

When asked how much he was willing to chip in, Arthur added: "I consider a gift for the furthering of God's work to be between me and God."

Arthur's statements were surprising, especially since jurors are forbidden by law in Canada from revealing what went on during deliberations and, traditionally, they do not indulge in post-mortems with reporters. Arthur's fellow jurors, having been awarded a daily jury fee of $85—$10 above the maximum —boarded a school bus back to the hotel to pick up their bags.

But Arthur chatted casually with a handful of reporters, nudged occasionally by a plainclothes RCMP officer standing beside him whenever the conversation strayed into forbidden territory.

Lest the public get the wrong idea, Arthur clarified his remarks in letters to major Alberta newspapers a week later.

"My intention is by no means to assist a 'defender of the faith' or to support anti-Semitism," he wrote. "My primary concern centres upon the issue of freedom of speech. While the specifics of the law, as established by Parliament, forced me to find Mr. Keegstra guilty of the offence in light of the facts presented, my firm conviction is that promotion of hatred and other related matters should never be brought before the courts."

Arthur said he had not intended to leave the impression "that I subscribe to all of the theories presented by Mr. Keegstra or that I approve of his interpretations of Christianity; I disagree with many of his views, but I am convinced that all new theories of history or religious views should be open to public consideration, regardless of how controversial they may be."

The Canadian Jewish community, which had feared an acquittal, was relieved at the verdict and unconcerned about the sentence.

"I'm a bit saddened that some people's belief is so vicious that the only way to protect other members of society is to bring criminal charges against them," said Alan Shefman of the B'nai B'rith.

Although he had expected a jail term, Shefman said the real benefit of the conviction was that 12 ordinary Canadians in a central Alberta community had found Keegstra guilty. Coupled with the Zundel conviction in Toronto, it showed ordinary Canadians, no matter what region of the country they lived in, weren't prepared to accept racist intolerance.

"I'm pleased with the verdict," added Len Dolgoy, a spokesman for Alberta's 12,000 Jews. "It goes beyond the Jewish community. All ethnic groups should be somewhat relieved that you can't teach hatred towards minority groups in schools."

The Jews were the targets, he said, but it could just as easily have been Blacks, Arabs, Catholics, Sikhs, native Indians or Pakistanis.

For the prosecution team, which had worked on the case almost 18 months, there was a sense of satisfaction.

A poker-faced Bruce Fraser said he was elated at the verdict. He would consider whether to recommend appealing the sentence after reviewing MacKenzie's pre-sentence comments. But like the Jewish observers, Fraser felt the conviction more important, expressing society's opposition to hate promotion.

"I see a point in bringing all this out, in dealing with it and not letting it fester underneath," he said. "I think that's what's been done here through the process. I don't think there is a penalty that'll deter him."

Giving Keegstra a platform was part of the process, even if it publicized his views to potential supporters.

"There's some people that, no matter what happens, he'll be a hero," said Fraser. "I think it was well worth it to expose him for what he was, what these students had to endure."

Back at Keegstra's headquarters there was no second-guessing, either. Relaxing with Christie on the front lawn on the rented house with some reporters, he had no regrets on their strategy.

When deliberations stretched into the fourth day Christie said he began thinking about the prospect of a hung jury.

"I was pretty convinced they couldn't make the decision at all," he said. "It said to me it was very likely there was an impossibility of a verdict."

It was plain the jury believed Keegstra was an honest man who held his beliefs sincerely, said Christie. His conclusion: the jury convicted under pressure or because of emotions. As well, the judge's directive that freedom of speech was not an issue might also have played a part.

After the verdict, the sentence became irrelevant, Christie felt.

"I didn't think of sentencing because I wasn't prepared to accept a conviction."

MacKenzie's charitable comments in his pre-sentence statement gave Keegstra the impression the judge was on his side.

"I think he is basically for freedom of speech, but I think he is caught in the system, too," said Keegstra.

But he had no kind words for Arthur, other than pity.

"I guess I'm different than most people; I feel sorry for the fellow." Keegstra said Arthur was put into a tough situation and didn't "have the moral character to do what was right."

Keegstra toyed with the idea of refusing to pay the fine, risking a six-month jail term for the default.

"It is a legal option," he said. "Greater men than I have done it."

But more likely was the prospect of an appeal, at least if Keegstra could raise the money to finance it. Besides Christie's discounted fee, legal costs could make an appeal prohibitive. One source in the Attorney General's Department said the cost alone of the required transcript of the 70-day trial is estimated at between $20,000 and $30,000.

Legal experts were reluctant to talk about the possible appeal grounds before an application was filed, but believed Keegstra and Christie would have the best chance of appealing what was for them the central theme of the case—freedom of speech.

With a conviction, Quigley's ruling became open to Keegstra for appeal. One lawyer who observed the trial said MacKenzie's rulings would provide little grist for an appeal and higher courts are reluctant to overturn jury verdicts without proof the trial judge had made substantial errors in law.

In mid-August Christie filed an application before the Alberta Court of Appeal to have the verdict overturned or a new trial ordered. He cited 32 grounds, including a repetition of those points Quigley had rejected at the pre-trial hearing. The remaining points dealt with trial evidence, testimony and rulings by MacKenzie, as well as aspects of MacKenzie's final instructions to the jury, and had all, at one time or another, been raised by Christie during the trial.

Christie also appealed the sentence, arguing that the fine was excessive considering sentences imposed for Criminal Code offences of similar seriousness. He also said MacKenzie had not sufficiently considered Keegstra's good character and the honesty with which he held his beliefs.*

*This was the situation up to press time (August, 1985).

# 11
# Send in the Scribes

*Accustom your children constantly to this; if a thing happened at one window and they say, when relating it, that it happened at another, do not let it pass . . . you do not know where deviation from truth will end.*

—Samuel Johnson

A news story about the firing of a teacher in a small, out-of-the-way community is not one to grab the attention of the media. The events that were to burgeon into the Keegstra affair were little noted at the time, but like a stone thrown into still waters, they set up ripples that were to wash against many shores and rock more than one boat.

Before things ended, the small town of Eckville was to squirm under the glare of publicity that extended to the national scene and beyond to the pages of the *New York Times*. Tempers would flare—one reporter seeking an interview found himself flung bodily from the door of an Eckville home—and residents would plead for an escape to obscurity.

Eventually, Eckville purged itself of its unwanted guests, but only after it had been portrayed as a community of red-necks and insular bigots. The presence of Jim Keegstra and his peculiar beliefs became a brand on Eckville, where image and substance became confused and where sympathy was sometimes mistaken for zealotry.

The beginning was almost unnoticed, like a small cloud on the horizon that may presage mere heat lightning or a full-fledged thunderstorm. The news stories in early December 1982 said Keegstra, a teacher at the Eckville Junior-Senior High School, had been fired by the local school board for persisting in teaching a vaguely anti-Semitic curriculum. The firing stories were followed by reports of student protests over the dismissal. Keegstra was portrayed as a popular teacher who might have had strange ideas, but who was well-liked.

He was mayor of the little community, a respected church-goer and a friend to many. Newspaper and broadcast stations began to send reporters to delve into Eckville, its people, its values and its curious former teacher.

Keegstra's firing, the loss of his appeal, his bickering with the Social Credit party, all were parts of a whole that never seemed to take shape. The Keegstra story was a jigsaw puzzle where all the pieces seemed the same color.

One problem may have been that few actually grasped the magnitude or scope of his ideas and his teachings. It became a handy shorthand to say that Keegstra had been fired for teaching that the extent of the Holocaust had been exaggerated. Reporters visited Eckville again and again. They talked with the residents, many of whom were growing increasingly exasperated with the unlooked-for publicity that lit the community in strobe-like flashes. Few of these people had any idea of what had really gone on in Keegstra's classes; few claimed to be familiar with his strident arguments against the Jewish "conspiracy."

The story twisted and turned. Eckville students went to Germany and visited Dachau. Premier Peter Lougheed made a statement in the legislature pleading for tolerance. A provincial committee was named to study tolerance and understanding. The Alberta Teachers' Association agonized over what to do about Keegstra.

In the fall of 1983, almost a year after the first stories were published, Keegstra stood for election as mayor. He had been acclaimed to the post for his first term when no other candidate stood for election and this would be his first test at the polls.

Media gathered as if to chronicle the election of a major political figure. Television cameras, newspaper reporters, photographers, broadcasters and the national news services all appeared. Then Keegstra was crushed when voters turned out en masse to reject him as mayor.

There would be more attention focused on the community over the next two years, but the suggestion of community support was gone, buried at the ballot box. There was a lasting bitterness in Eckville, though, against news reports that were seen as unfair.

J. P. O'Callaghan, publisher of the *Calgary Herald* and former head of the Canadian Daily Newspaper Publishers Association, said some of the media may indeed have used the coverage of the Keegstra affair to reinforce old stereotypes.

"It's a popular myth in central Canada that there's nothing but red-neck ranchers out here."

Were the people of Eckville really portrayed as bigoted bumpkins? Steve Hume, editor of the *Edmonton Journal*, argued they were not: "Any thinking, reasonable person would realize you can't stereotype an entire community on one fool's thinking."

Hume said he had no doubts that some in Eckville did share Keegstra's ideas, but "you can't tar the entire community."

The Zundel trial in Toronto took the headlines early in 1985, and the news coverage, especially the stories about the Holocaust being a hoax, caused soul-searching among some of the media. It was probably the first time that such a sensitive topic, so anguishing to so many people, had been played out in a Canadian courtroom. The subject matter was so wide and the testimony so startling, that some media outlets began self-examinations over the handling of the trial. They also looked ahead to Keegtra's trial, which promised more of the same.

The dilemma that had editors brooding was probably summed up in the post-trial photograph of a grinning Zundel, complete with hard hat, being hoisted on the shoulders of triumphant supporters. He seemed to be smiling right at the newspapers and television stations that had given him an unprecedented platform.

Editors knew that the reporting and headlines had caused pain and suffering in the Jewish community. The questions about the reality of the Holocaust, the obscene suggestions that Auschwitz was a summer camp with dance floors and swimming pools, the testimony of self-styled experts who argued about the source of fuel for the crematoria left people shaken. In the newsrooms, it was clear the Keegstra trial would dredge up similar material and more, and would give Keegstra the same kind of forum Zundel had had—Zundel who crowed after his trial that he could not have purchased the publicity for a million dollars.

Delegations from the Jewish community talked with senior editors of some news organizations. Their concern was that the testimony in the Keegstra trial, however cruel, would effectively be carried unquestioned in news stories. They wanted to see Keegstra's views contrasted with generally accepted historical fact. That left the editors in another quandary. To take that approach might leave reporters usurping the role of the jury, which is the sole arbiter of fact in the courtroom. To bring out contradictory evidence not heard in court could leave reporters open to legal sanctions. It might even be grounds for a mistrial. The request from the Jewish community was turned down, in full knowledge that the news stories from the Red Deer court-house were bound to be offensive, at least in part. It was Hob-son's choice, that is, no choice at all.

The dilemma for reporters and editors was clear. Could they just ignore the case? No. Here was a trial that would address a matter of obvious social concern. If only to demonstrate that Keegstra was being treated fairly, the case would have to be covered. Could the evidence be toned down, bowdlerized or even ignored? Again, the answer was no. To sweep Keegstra's ideas under the rug would be a disservice. Painful as it might be, the bitter, demeaning testimony had to be reported.

The principles were clear enough, but the emotional impact was obvious. That side of the question was aired in a letter to the editor of the Red Deer *Advocate* published about two weeks into the trial. The letter, signed by six members of the clergy of different denominations, asked that the trial be played down: "We recognize that in the trial of Jim Keegstra, the press has an obligation to cover the proceedings adequately to satisfy the need and right of the public to know the facts." The letter went on to urge moderation: "We urge you to avoid giving undue prominence to this story lest you convey the impression that revisionist views are, or ought to be, seriously regarded by any significant segment of Canadian people. Treat the case as you might treat any minor legal action and this will allow these revisionists to disappear into the obscurity they so richly deserve."

The trial, however, was not a "minor legal action." If con-victed, Keegstra faced up to two years in jail. It was not a traffic ticket, nor could it be treated as such.

Mel Sufrin, vice-president for editorial operations for The Canadian Press, the national news-gathering co-operative, saw the problem clearly. He is a Jew and a life-long newsman. However sympathetic he might be to the argument that Keeg-stra's views were hurtful, he could not agree to the idea that reporters go out of their way to question so-called facts pre-sented at the trial.

"When you get into a trial before a jury, it's very difficult for a reporter to get involved with . . . taking issue with incorrect facts." The problem is the same in every trial, although the issues were magnified far beyond the normal in the Keegstra trial. The adversarial system of justice means that proceedings tend to sound one-sided. The Crown presents its case, the defence cross-examines. The defence takes its turn, the Crown cross-examines.

"It's completely out of whack at different times," said Sufrin. The problem for reporters is that they are required, legally and ethically, to provide a fair and honest account of the proceedings. If days of testimony favor one side over another, then the reporting of that testimony is bound to appear one-sided. When the other side presents its case, the balance shifts again.

"When Keegstra was being questioned, you had weeks of distorted views being presented," said Sufrin.

Norm Webster, editor-in-chief of the Toronto *Globe and Mail*, agreed it was impossible for reporters to intrude into the evidence.

"I don't think we can get involved in interpolating or interpreting matters in a trial," Webster said. "I think there would be legal difficulties with that."

Despite these concerns about usurping the function of the jury in correcting some of Keegstra's "facts," there were times when common sense forced some clarifications. For instance, Keegstra stated flatly that the Rockefeller family of Standard Oil fame was Jewish and that the patriarch, John D., was a Sephardic Jew from Portugal.

That was so far-out that some news organizations, after talking to their lawyers, decided to point out in their stories that the Rockefellers have always said they were Baptists and have been accepted as such for years. The same thing happened when Keegstra suggested that Franklin Delano Roosevelt shot himself after Josef Stalin told him he could not be president of the world. Official records and the physicians who were there say Roosevelt died of a cerebral hemorrhage.

But there were so many other things that could not be corrected. To take issue with the whole conspiracy was obviously impossible. To correct Keegstra's statements about the Talmud (he said the Talmud allows Jews to cheat Gentiles, kill them and even have sex with young girls) was also a problem. To begin a debate on the meaning of the Talmud, a study which involves some scholars for their entire lives, was also impossible. Despite the galling testimony, despite puzzled telephone calls from readers, the reporters were helpless. Caught between their commitment to a fair and honest account of the testimony and the legal niceties which prevent wide-open rebuttals of evidence, the media had to grit their teeth and keep on.

In most trials, if there is a dispute over some fact, it might be fairly simple to go to a conventional source of information, be it an almanac, encyclopedia or a standard reference book, look up the matter in dispute and publish the "correct" answer. But in this trial, the references themselves were basically on trial, because Keegstra said they were all censored by the conspiracy. By trying to correct Keegstra, reporters would be getting into the very question before the court.

Still, the trial had to be covered in detail, although newspapers looked for ways to ease the painful impact of some of the evidence in the ways in which they handled the stories.

In newspapers, the question of where to run a story is almost as important as the decision to cover it. In the Keegstra case, Hume said, it was decided that major legal and constitutional matters would receive prominent play while other material, including "tedious arguments over revisionist views" would be run inside the paper. Of the more than 90 stories *The Journal* ran during the course of the trial, only about five per cent were front-page stories, said Hume.

Webster of *The Globe and Mail* said the same thing. He said there were concerns that the Zundel case had been overplayed in the newspaper and while the Keegstra trial would receive coverage, it was not going to be overdone.

O'Callaghan of *The Herald* agreed, adding that the trial story did not have to be overplayed: "I think it was one of those stories that generates its own momentum."

So the news ground on. Keegstra spent 26 days on the stand recounting his oddball views and a handful of news organizations stuck through all 15 weeks of the proceedings. They included The Canadian Press, its broadcasting affiliate, Broadcast News Ltd., *The Journal*, *The Herald*, *The Advocate*, the Canadian Broadcasting Corp., radio, television and French service, and Central Alberta broadcasters such as CKRD Red Deer. As well, there was a smattering of other media representatives, including a reporter from the *Canadian Jewish News*.

For some, the trial was an easier chore than others. Television, for example, was caught in a situation where visuals—the key to the medium—are very limited. Beyond stock shots of people filing into the courtroom, and artists' drawings, there is little to show in a trial. CBC's national television network covered the early portion of the trial, returned for some of Keegstra's testimony and was there for the end. Local reporters kept an eye on things while the national network was not on hand.

As the trial ground on, debates continued in the various newsrooms over the handling of the stories and their contents.

From the other side of the coin, there were complaints.

Christie claimed the media had condemned his client without trial. The lawyer was bitter about the news coverage of the story, even though he and Keegstra had refused to ask for a ban on coverage of the preliminary hearing in 1984. Such bans, routine in Canada, are designed to ensure that the impartiality of potential jurors is not tainted by undue media exposure of a case. The Canadian Criminal Code allows the accused to seek a ban, but Christie had not done so.

Christie sought to have a mistrial declared over various news stories, a motion the court rejected. Christie complained specifically about a story by Robert Lee published in *Saturday Night* magazine. The piece, entitled "Keegstra's Children" was published in May. Lee, a former Red Deer *Advocate* reporter, was working for the now-defunct United Press Canada in Edmonton when he wrote the story.

Keegstra, on the other hand, said news coverage of the trial was fair. He seemed caught in a contradiction of his dealings with reporters. He was often open and candid with individual reporters, even though he professed to believe the media were controlled by Jews and were part of his world conspiracy.

What of the Jewish community, who had their sacred books reviled, their reputations besmirched and their history denied? Alan Shefman, national director of field services for the League of Human Rights of B'nai B'rith, and Manuel Prutschi, national director of community relations for the Canadian Jewish Congress, saw the trial and conviction as a fair trade-off.

"I think that's a worthwhile price to pay," said Prutschi.

Shefman said he did not think the widespread reporting of the trial and of Keegstra's ideas would make much difference as far as making Keegstra converts was concerned.

"That, I think, goes to the good sense and judgment of Canadians, that they're not willing to accept this crap."

Many of the media, though, had personal doubts about the wisdom of laying the charges in the first place. Freedom of expression is bread and butter, life itself, to reporters and editors, and there were many who thought Keegstra's ideas, however repugnant they might be, deserved to stand or fall in the marketplace, without criminal charges.

After all, he had been yanked out of the classroom, prohibited from teaching and stripped of his job as mayor. Why not leave him to rummage through his books and pamphlets and tracts in peace? After all, the media reports had, in effect, carried much of what he was being tried for saying.

It was the kind of question that will be debated around press clubs and in quiet newsrooms at night for years to come. And, as with so many other questions debated in the same forums, there will likely be as many answers as there are participants.

# 12

# The Students of Doubt

---

*Wisdom is the principal thing; therefore get wisdom; and with all thy getting, get understanding.*

—Proverbs 3:7

---

Cain Ramstead sat in the living room of his parents' comfortable home on the corner lot not far from the school. The ordeal of his testimony now past, he considered his career prospects. He had a summer job as a lot boy at a Red Deer car dealership. The thought of a second year at the journalism course he was taking had palled.

He had looked into a career in law enforcement, but the job market was poor. A photography buff, he began thinking about becoming a television cameraman, like the ones who surrounded Keegstra on his way out of the courthouse at the end of the trial.

"I'm just as glad he didn't go to jail," said Ramstead. "When you start putting men like Jim Keegstra in jail, who's next?"

Ramstead still holds Keegstra in immense regard. He stood out, Ramstead said, because he seemed genuinely concerned about the students' welfare at a time when the school was drifting and the teachers seemed apathetic.

"None of the teachers cared what you did," Ramstead said, echoing other pupils on both sides of the Keegstra issue.

Whatever people thought about Keegstra's ideas, Ramstead maintained few were unaware of them.

"It wasn't like it was some little secret," he said. "The whole bloody town knew about it."

Yet, he said, people were prepared to accept what some students called "Mr. Keegstra's crazy ideas" because of all the good they felt he otherwise accomplished. It was certainly true of his final class, for whom the firing came as a bolt from the blue.

"Everybody was just wild," Ramstead remembered. "Had [school superintendent Robert David] walked into that room, he would have had a very nasty reception."

Ramstead insisted students had to learn Keegstra's theory for tests and essays, but were never forced to accept it. Nevertheless, Keegstra's opinions about the manipulation of history books and the influence of Jews still strike the young man as plausible. Subsequent reading has reinforced that view.

Keegstra's dismissal and prosecution left Ramstead suspicious and defensive. He had planned to embark on a teaching career, a vocation he now saw as poisoned.

"Never, ever, ever again," he said. "What if I slip up and say something? I might land in jail."

Ramstead has become identified with Keegstra's views. He felt himself on trial almost as much as his former teacher.

"To me it seemed like [Fraser] was out to get me," Ramstead said of his testimony. "That was without a doubt the hardest mental work I've ever done in my life; keeping on guard."

When his connection to the Keegstra case became public knowledge, Ramstead said he was cursed by a Jew in Calgary. But his own first encounters with Jews, the first he had met outside Keegstra's teachings, left him with the impression they were no different from anybody else.

"I don't hold any grudge against Jews."

Blair Andrew did some serious thinking, said his mother Marg, who had two daughters and a son go through Keegstra's social studies courses.

Blair had accepted a lot of what Keegstra said as fact. Now, his mother said, he was doing some reading on his own, but remained confused about some things. With the trial over, the whole family would like nothing better than to see a pyre made from the class's notes and essays, she said.

Kelly Cordon took Keegstra's class in 1979-80. He said Keegstra saw the Jews behind nearly every malevolent act in history and Cordon accepted it because Keegstra never suggested it was anything but true.

*Cain Ramstead was in the last social studies class taught by Keegstra. He still believes many of the things he learned about the power of a Jewish conspiracy. (Canadian Press photo)*

*Marg Andrew, whose son and two daughters took social studies from Keegstra, was part of a group that started complaining about his teachings, especially those concerning Roman Catholics, in the late 1970s. (Canadian Press photo)*

"I felt like it was about the gospel truth," Cordon recalled. "There was not a shadow of a doubt that what he was saying was true."

Despite Keegstra's assertions to the contrary, Cordon said he got the impression his teacher admired Hitler for his fight against the Jews, which in the context of the course was justified.

Then Cordon, whose testimony was pivotal in the Crown's case, encountered reality in the form of some elderly Dutch men and women who lived at the Red Deer nursing home. As he worked there on weekends they recounted their experiences under Nazi occupation.

"A lot of those people had horrible stories to tell," said Cordon. "There's no way that I can doubt that. That's what really changed my mind."

Four children of Harry and Violet Safron were taught by Keegstra, under a climate of a cold war that lasted some five years. The Safrons, an industrious farm family who live just west of Eckville, began complaining in 1976 about the anti-Catholic tone of Keegstra's social studies classes.

They found themselves fobbed off with suggestions that perhaps they should try to sneak a tape recorder into the classroom. Danny, the eldest, and Terry found themselves foils for Keegstra's cutting remarks about their religion, all in the context of historical analysis.

"It was just like with the Jews," said Violet Safron. "He took it from history. He just seemed to assume that you were like this from history."

Daughter Brenda, the youngest, joined her two brothers in Keegstra's bad books because she defied him. She spent two-thirds of the year in the hallway, her mother said.

Only Dennis, Terry's younger brother, seemed to fare well with Keegstra and still defends his former teacher. Dennis became good friends with Larry Keegstra, the eldest son, and once took him to visit the Catholic church at nearby Sylvan Lake. The younger Keegstra, now a fundamentalist minister, had never set foot inside one before, according to Dennis Safron. They remained friends, despite Jim Keegstra's disapproval, and drifted apart only as the paths of their lives diverged. Dennis still considers what Keegstra taught him about the conspiracy a valid matter for debate. Just who does run the country's banking system and why is so much of what we read in newspapers and see on television distorted and inaccurate? Most of all: why was Keegstra suddenly fired?

"If Jim is so bad, why was he allowed to teach for so many years?"

Terry has no such questions. The brash young man, who at 25 owned a small construction firm, could not escape the thought Keegstra harbored a resentment of his family's prosperity. The Safrons took advantage of opportunities, such as opening a kind of summer farm camp for city children. Mrs. Safron, for a time, worked in the local bank. The family was always well-turned-out, but had always worked for it, said Harry Safron. Yet the appearance of being well-to-do seemed to bother Keegstra, said Terry.

"He mentioned that more than once, the wealth of the family," said Terry. "He had the attitude that farmers were very wealthy." The Safrons had also committed the unpardonable sin of buying Soviet-built tractors.

Terry recalled Keegstra's reaction when he arrived at school his last year with a brand-new, $16,000 four-wheel-drive truck, paid for with money he had earned over the summer working on the oil rigs and putting his salary into interest-bearing term deposits.

"He made an example of me because I used the bank's interest to further myself in life," said Terry. " 'You're making money off nothing,' he said."

Danny, Terry and Brenda withstood the attacks on their self-esteem and the family now looks back on the time philosophically.

Dennis remembered that Keegstra expressed his views, but always invited students to prove him wrong—if they could.

Trouble was, no one could, Terry pointed out.

"Who's going to run up to Edmonton, to the university, to get some evidence to prove him wrong?"

There was a limit to how much skepticism Keegstra could accept. To push him to the wall was to be marked as a potentially disruptive influence and to be put in your place.

"He was a very sly man," said Terry. "It would almost look like you were asking for it. If you agreed with him, you were his buddy."

Marg Andrew said the children were not only misled, but cheated out of their rightful education.

"I think they missed a great deal," she said. "They don't really know how governments are run or a great deal about politics."

Keegstra's teachings bred in them a fear the system stacks the cards against them from the start.

"The kids that get away from Eckville, I think, are going to grow up a great deal," she said. "For the kids that never leave, I don't know what's going to happen."

Both the Safrons and the Andrews were upset about the sense of insecurity Keegstra seemed to leave in Catholic children over their religion.

"In a public school I don't think you should have to defend that in front of your classmates," said Marg Andrew.

Dr. Brendan Rule, a University of Alberta social psychologist who was to testify for the Crown at Keegstra's trial, said there is little scientific data on how much lasting impact Keegstra's teachings might have on his former students. There are only laboratory experiments, and experiences with wartime brainwashing, to go by. They show the effects could last a long time.

Keegstra was in perhaps the best position to have a lasting effect, Rule said. He was highly respected as a teacher and well-liked by his students. He also concentrated on instilling attitudes and values.

"It's a bit different from rote memorization of text material," she said. "If a person is an expert, or well-liked, they will have a big impact on acceptance."

Keegstra's methods of teaching, the use of classroom discussion, essays and tests also helped plant his ideas more deeply because he got the students involved.

"It increases the likelihood that people's attitudes will change," Rule said.

The age of the students was probably not an important factor in Keegstra's success, she said. They weren't at a particularly susceptible age, but they were in a particularly susceptible environment.

Based on this, the line that separates Jim Keegstra from any other imaginative, enthusiastic teacher is pretty thin. The same things that made Keegstra an effective propagandist for the Jewish conspiracy theory also enliven countless other classrooms with much more innocent debate. Eckville principal Edwin Olsen said he found nothing disturbing in what Keegstra taught because he thought, perhaps naively, that Keegstra was drawing out his students, making them think, piquing their interest in social studies.

Critics of the province's education system have called for revisions in the social studies curriculum, which they say was allowed to become too broad and flexible in the 1970s.

The provincial Committee on Tolerance and Understanding recommended attacking the problem more broadly by developing a policy which would encourage an overall acceptance of minorities and encourage children to appreciate Canada's cultural diversity.

The committee, which received almost 500 briefs over its 18-month investigation, said in its 200-page report the problem may have been illustrated by Keegstra's teachings in social studies, but the solution lay in updating Alberta's goals of education and schooling. The committee made some specific recommendations on promoting education about different cultures, including working with teachers and administrators to ensure awareness of multiculturalism, examining personal attitudes in the school system and increasing knowledge and skills in intercultural education. As well, teachers should be provided with the tools to deal with stereotyping, prejudice, discrimination, racism and bigotry in the classroom.

The education establishment must also still decide who is responsible for assessing teacher conduct in the class. School boards bridle at the thought of provincial education officials monitoring teachers, but the Alberta Teachers' Association, which after the Keegstra affair offered to take over the classroom evaluations, is considered by some to be the least equipped of the three bodies to judge its own.

The odds seem long against blowing the whistle on a Jim Keegstra, especially in a rural school. Rules of the association make it difficult for one teacher to criticize a colleague, and the association also reserves the right to take disciplinary action against its own, short of firing.

In rural school districts like the County of Lacombe, where school principals are full-time teachers as well as administrators, the district superintendent is responsible for teacher evaluation and fielding complaints.

Although it can be argued that a light should have gone on for Olsen when he saw the offending essays after the Ackerman complaint, he was technically correct in saying his responsibility had been discharged once Robert David was informed. Olsen points out that changes in school board policy have since then given him more responsibility in monitoring teachers.

Parents, too, must shoulder some of the blame. Marg Andrew believes many didn't know the full story about Keegstra's teachings because they didn't listen to their children, or simply didn't ask what they were doing in school. It's not uncommon in Eckville, or anywhere else, for parents, when they ask what Johnny did in school today, to be satisfied with the answer, "Oh, nothing."

"You put implicit faith in the education system," said Andrew.

The hand-wringing over education policy began well before Keegstra was brought to trial, so the question of benefits arising from the successful prosecution are more difficult to assess.

Neither Keegstra nor his supporters were swayed by the verdict, and the conviction gives no guarantee other hatemongers of whatever stripe will be cowed. The fact Keegstra's conviction was the first registered by a jury under the hate promotion statute—the others have been before judges alone—might encourage attorneys general elsewhere in Canada to go after the preachers of hate. The long-term outlook for any such trend rests on the outcome of a possible appeal in the Keegstra case.

Yet civil libertarians will likely remain uneasy.

If, as its framers hoped in the late 1960s, the law becomes a successful net to catch the hatemongers, might not the mesh also snare cherished freedoms at questionable cost?

Borovoy of the civil liberties association suggests that even if the law can be made to work, its effectiveness as a tool against hatred is questionable. West Germany currently has tough laws against disseminating hatred, especially dealing with Holocaust denial. But, as Borovoy is fond cf pointing out, pre-Hitler Germany also had tough laws against racial slurs which in many respects resemble Canadian legislation. During the 15 years of the Weimar Republic between the end of the First World War and the advent of the Nazi regime, there were about 200 court cases involving anti-Semitic speech. But it didn't stop the publication of Hitler's *Mein Kampf* nor the Jew-baiting conducted in the streets of Germany by Nazi bullyboys.

Attorney General Crawford sees no alternative but to enforce the law if there are grounds for a charge. "I can't change the view that a law, when passed by Parliament . . . if there is sufficient evidence, it should normally be the subject of a charge," he says.

If the law has any value, it may be as an official demonstration that society will not tolerate public promotion of hatred. If that is so, Borovoy wonders whether society is not better served by leaving the Keegstras of Canada to wallow in the obscurity they deserve rather than giving them a platform to espouse their hatred. Canadians daily make their choice. Most reject the hatemongers; the rest likely won't be dissuaded by legal sanctions, only driven underground.

What about the man on whom the consequences weigh most heavily? He has no second thoughts about what he taught his students: Christian love, a healthy skepticism for the conventional view of things, a wariness of the Hidden Hand. There's no danger his teachings might translate into violence.

"The students were told bluntly, that you do not go out and kill, you do not go out and destroy," said Keegstra. "What you do is go out and inform. You go out and bring out knowledge, bring out truth, and in that way we keep those people who want to consolidate power from consolidating it.

"However, at the same time, if they see people or groups of people in a conspiracy forming that wants an overdose of power, then they ought to do something about that."

He added he was talking about political action to "get the right man elected."

Was he not concerned he had equipped each of his students with a ready-made excuse on which to blame the ills of the world, even their personal failures?

"They were taught to be responsible for every action they partook in," he said. "They would one day be called to account."

But, he agreed, his students, especially the ones who had to testify at the trial, now might be marked for life by the conspiracy.

In his ability to compartmentalize his thinking, Keegstra insists he is neither an anti-Semite—because there no longer is such a thing as a Semitic Jew—or a white supremacist, which he considers simply the other side of the Chosen People myth.

"They're as racist and bigoted, generally, as Zionist Jews

are," he said. "How on earth could you go along with something like that, just changing the horses, but promoting the same philosophy?"

Yet he acknowledges he has become a tool of groups like the neo-Nazis surrounding Zundel and the Aryan Nations Church, both of which sent representatives to the trial. Even John Ross Taylor, the 70-year-old war horse of the Canadian white supremacist movement, sat through much of the trial before disappearing mysteriously near the end. Whether he approved or not, this group attached themselves to the train of Keegstra's notoriety, for the most part riding free.

"I can't stop them," said Keegstra. "How can I? If people want to listen to what I have to say, they'll find what I have to say is different."

One question nagged. If this was such a ruthless conspiracy, not above assassination and massacre throughout its history, why had it allowed Keegstra a public platform for more than two years, to rail against its machinations, however fruitlessly? If, as Keegstra believed, the conspiracy was aware of the threat he presented as a teacher, why had it not quietly done away with him, perhaps a car accident on one of the hilly country roads around Eckville?

"Scapegoats are very important," Keegstra figures. "Platform? That doesn't hurt them any. Do you really think that this platform they're giving me is going to hurt them one iota?

"We've got so many apathetic and stupid people out there. I'm just a little fish, man. I don't amount to nothing."

# Index